# SOLUTION-FOCUSED
# SCHOOLS:
# ANTI-BULLYING
# AND BEYOND

*Sue Young*

First published September 2009
Second Edition February 2010

Published by BT Press
17 Avenue Mansions, Finchley Road, London NW3 7AX
www.btpress.co.uk
+44 (0)20 7794 4495

Front cover illustration by Tahera Choudhury,
Thoresby Primary School, Hull

Designed by Alex Gollner

ISBN 978-1-871697-80-3

# CONTENTS

# ACKNOWLEDGEMENTS

I wish to acknowledge all the staff and pupils that I have enjoyed working alongside in schools – too numerous to mention by name, although some can be found in the examples in this book.

Several colleagues in particular have been a constant source of support. Dez Allenby was my line manager when I first began to adopt a solution-focused approach; he instinctively recognises the value of listening intently and giving positive feedback to all his staff. Gail Holdorf shared my passion for using solution-focused practice in anti-bullying work and became a close colleague and friend. Alec Williams encouraged me through the writing of an earlier book *Solutions to Bullying*, of which this is an updated and extended version.

My training in particular has benefited enormously from watching and working alongside Yasmin Ajmal and Guy Shennan from BRIEF in London. In the couple of years before her death, Insoo Kim Berg recommended my work and asked me to contribute to the third edition of *Interviewing for Solutions* – I was just one of the many people she inspired and encouraged.

While writing this book, I have exercised the patience of a number of friends – for their kindness I would like to thank Janet Lloyd, John Holland and Gail Holdorf. During later drafts, Ben Furman, Dez Allenby and Guy Shennan were all generous with their time and offered many thought-provoking and helpful comments.

Finally, and most importantly, it would never have been finished without the steadfast support of Kerstin Måhlberg & Maud Sjöblom.

# FIRST
# FOREWORD

*Yasmin Ajmal*

Anyone who has ever worked with Sue Young or heard her speak cannot have failed to witness her dedication: her belief in her colleagues; her desire for every student to enjoy a safe and nurturing school environment; and her trust in the ability of all those involved with young people, including the young people themselves, to achieve this.

Over the past decade she has distilled her passion and belief into this book.

The beauty of Anti-bullying and beyond is the direct and concise way in which it encourages the development of methods that create an environment incompatible with bullying. Sue's work draws on the talents and values that already exist in each school, and the plethora of ideas that pour off its pages are just as applicable at a whole school level as in individual cases. It dovetails into a strong and rigorous approach.

Young people are a woefully underused resource, with boundless energy and the best instincts to find their way through the maze of growing up. Sue illustrates time and again, with rich case studies, how to identify and utilize these strengths.

I remember at our first meeting, Sue's amazement at just how effective her work with support groups had been. She has since transformed this achievement into a lucid and practical set of ideas that will be of interest to anyone who wants to ensure that schools are safe and nurturing places for our children.

Brief, London
VSO, Zanzibar

# Second
# Foreword

*Kerstin Måhlberg & Maud Sjöblom*

We are highly delighted to find that Sue Young is breaking new ground, taking the solution-focused approach one step further by applying it to achieving potential, rather than just to solving problems. This will become accepted thinking.

There has been concern about bullying in schools for several decades. Despite it being one of the principal causes for children to feel unhappy in school, there is too little in the field of research about how to put an end to bullying. Most methods adopted against bullying are problem-based and there is insufficient evaluation of the effects. Therefore this updated version of Sue's work is particularly welcome.

*Solution-Focused Schools: Anti-bullying and beyond* provides a powerful set of principles and strategies that will transform the whole educational approach to dealing with bullying. This is the most extensive work on taking a solution-focused approach to bullying and will change practice and open up new ways for schools to develop cooperation among pupils as a basis for building friendship and safety in schools.

Sue brings a wide repertoire of knowledge and first hand experience to her work, especially her development of support groups. Her track record gives her work credibility. We are enchanted by the simplicity and astounded by the outcomes. We appreciate the clear step-by-step explanations.

Whatever the causes of students' behaviour, schools need effective ways of dealing with bullying. This book focuses on just that. It is extremely important that children do not feel excluded by criticism or guilt, and this book provides an approach that inherently promotes self-reliance.

The overwhelming majority of pupils want a peaceful, safe and happy place to learn. Every parent wants their child to be safe in school. This programme works in that direction. Parental involvement is now an integral part of school life and this will continue to be ever more important in future years.

The approach in this book promotes a climate of cooperation, hope and heart within the whole-school setting and will help us to keep our children safe and happy in school. Sue Young's book needs to be read by anyone interested in being in the forefront of the development of solution-focused schools.

*Kerstin Måhlberg*, Headteacher of FKC Mellansjö School, special
  educationalist, trainer.
*Maud Sjöblom,* special educationalist, supervisor, trainer.
Co-authors: Solution-Focused Education – for a happier school
  www.lip4u.se
  www.sfe4u.org

# INTRODUCTION

This book is about developing a new way of working to address the longstanding problem of bullying in schools. Solution-focused ideas were first discovered in a therapeutic setting for families in the USA by Steve de Shazer and Insoo Kim Berg. Since their pioneering work of the late 1970s and early 1980s, solution-focused ideas have been applied in ever-wider contexts.

As a result of this broader understanding of the relevance of solution-focused practice, we are now seeing the emergence of schools describing themselves as 'solution-focused'. In a solution-focused school, the staff are able to bring about change by being motivated, not by the need to solve problems, but by the desire to realise the potential of all their pupils.

The solution-focused approach can be used whenever change for the better is wanted, in whatever area. Although this book concentrates on anti-bullying in schools, solution-focused thinking has important applications wherever one wants to encourage positive change. Within an educational context, this could be in raising attainment, improving an area of the curriculum or developing the school as a centre of the community – these would all be commendable. Anti-bullying provides an example of how solution-focused conversations can facilitate change at every level of school organisation. These conversations are powerful and creative in terms of developing supportive, happy and successful schools.

Bullying is a matter of common concern – it figures highly in children's and parents' worries, particularly at transition points in schooling. At best, bullying may cause temporary unhappiness in school; at worst it can contribute to serious mental health difficulties. The prime aims of schooling include preparing children for adulthood by fulfilling their potential as responsible and caring citizens and helping them develop the resilience to cope with the general buffeting and difficulties life has in store.

The values promoted in school are important because they influence the society our children will inherit. Allowing bullying to take place implicitly condones the abuse of weaker members of the school community (including staff and parents) by those who are physically or psychologically stronger. Not only is this detrimental to vulnerable children but it ultimately brutalises some children who bully others and provides them with a false sense of empowerment that they may carry into their adult lives.

The first chapter outlines how solution-focused practice can bring a new perspective to promoting change and make anti-bullying in schools more effective. The second chapter describes how professional development at the whole-school level can support a safe, supportive and friendly ethos, before applying the same principles in the third chapter to working with pupils in the classroom. The fourth chapter introduces more general considerations when responding to incidents of bullying, followed in detail in the fifth and sixth chapters respectively by two different solution-focused strategies – peer support groups and individual interviewing. Examples taken from practice are interspersed throughout the text. Where cases concerning individuals have been described, names and other details have been changed to ensure confidentiality unless otherwise acknowledged.

The aspiration in solution-focused schools is not simply to reduce bullying, but to create an environment incompatible with it. By recognising and nurturing the strengths of all their pupils, including those of friendship and support, solution-focused schools promote these life-skills to the benefit of their pupils' families and the wider community, ultimately contributing to an emotionally healthy society.

# CHAPTER 1
# TOWARDS SOLUTION-FOCUSED ANTI-BULLYING

## Introduction

This chapter outlines how anti-bullying has so far largely taken a problem-solving approach, following the pioneering work by Olweus in Scandinavia, despite equivocal results. Although 'whole-school' programmes usually demand a high level of additional staff input and pupil involvement and may take a year or more to implement, there have been doubts raised concerning their effectiveness. Moreover there is no clear agreement from the research about which elements of anti-bullying interventions reduce bullying, or more worryingly, appear to increase it. This chapter describes how an alternative, solution-focused approach was first discovered and developed in a therapeutic setting and later applied in schools, especially to help pupils with behaviour difficulties. More recently, teachers have realised solution-focused ideas have a wider relevance in schools than simply helping pupils or staff with problems. It is suggested that a solution-focused perspective invites a radically different approach to anti-bullying and provides a means of identifying a more effective way forward.

## Traditional anti-bullying campaigns in schools

Bullying has always been a feature of school life but national anti-bullying programmes have a relatively short history. Olweus was conducting research into bullying, particularly in Sweden, when he was asked to work on the first national campaign in Norway in 1983 following public concern arising from the suicides of three schoolboys. At the start of the project, Olweus conducted the first large-scale survey of bullying with questionnaires to 130,000 pupils, aged 8 to 16.

He found that about 15% of students were involved in bullying 'with some regularity', either as bullies (7%) or victims (9%). About 5% were involved, as bullies or victims or both, in 'more serious bullying problems', i.e. occurring about once a week, or more frequently. From this survey he concluded, 'bullying was (and still is, according to more recent and less comprehensive surveys) a considerable problem in Norwegian schools and affects a very large number of students' (Olweus, 1999, p. 32-33). Subsequent surveys of pupils in other countries, including Sweden, Finland, England, USA, Canada, The Netherlands, Japan, Ireland, Spain and Australia have indicated a similar or greater prevalence. Thus within the last 20 years, bullying in schools has become an issue of international concern and countries throughout the world have begun campaigns against bullying, greatly influenced by the first anti-bullying programme of Olweus.

In England for example, the first specific anti-bullying guidance, *Action against Bullying* (Johnstone, Munn & Edwards, 1991) previously issued in Scotland, was circulated to schools in 1992. At this time, the government was already funding a large research project, led by Smith in Sheffield, culminating in advice for all schools, *Bullying – Don't Suffer in Silence: An anti-bullying pack for schools* (DFE, 1994). The *School Standards and Framework Act 1998* made anti-bullying policies a legal requirement of schools and *The Race Relations (Amendment) Act 2000* required any incidents of racist bullying to be recorded. A revised edition of the Sheffield anti-bullying pack was made available to schools in 2000 and in 2002 the government funded the *Anti-Bullying Alliance* and appointed regional co-ordinators to bring together the work of over 60 different organisations.

In 2003 Ofsted, the school inspection authority, issued advice in *Bullying: effective action in secondary schools*. The following year, a high-profile government anti-bullying drive began, including TV, radio and poster advertising with celebrities from the world of music and sport. All schools were encouraged to sign up to *Bullying – A Charter for Action* and hold an annual, anti-bullying week, supported by resources for teachers and co-ordinated by the Anti-Bullying Alliance. In 2005, new national guidelines, *Bullying: policy and practice,* were issued and *SEAL (Social and Emotional Aspects of Learning)* was introduced into primary schools, including guidance and resource materials on the theme of *Say No to Bullying.* Completely revised government advice, *Safe to Learn* was introduced by the Department for Children, Schools and Families (DCSF) in 2007, supplemented in 2008 by guidance on homophobic bullying and bullying related to special educational needs and disabilities. *The National Healthy Schools Programme,* a joint initiative of the DCSF and the Department of Health, also produced guidance, most recently in conjuction with the Office of the Children's Commissioner and the Anti-Bullying Alliance, *Anti-bullying: Guidance for Schools,* in 2008.

This exponential growth in advice and resources for schools has been produced against a background of an equivalent expansion of research into bullying. Much of the early research explored the nature of bullying in schools, on the assumption that the more we know about it, the more we will be able to reduce it. 'First there must be some understanding of what bullying is, and why some children bully others, and why some children are bullied, before you can decide on a course of action' (Rigby, 1996, p. 2).

Consequently, various aspects of bullying have been studied, including the definition of bullying, its prevalence, different types and new forms of bullying, such as homophobic and 'cyber bullying', how bullying is age-related and/or gender related, the possible causes of bullying, negative effects, places where bullying tends to happen and groups that are particularly vulnerable. There is also an increasing interest in gathering children's and young people's own views on all aspects of bullying.

## Effectiveness of interventions

All the guidance, resources, research, projects and high-profile anti-bullying campaigns have both raised everyone's awareness about bullying and tried to offer schools effective responses. Nevertheless, despite all this activity in the last 20 years, there does not seem to be any lessening of anxiety about bullying in schools, let alone any perception that bullying is becoming less of a problem. Bullying remains a major source of concern and continues to feature frequently in education-related publications as well as in the general media.

Recently, some of the most respected researchers in the field have begun to raise doubts about the effectiveness of anti-bullying work. A comprehensive report prepared for the Swedish National Council for Crime Prevention by Ttofi, Farrington & Baldry (2008) reviewed 30 anti-bullying intervention studies worldwide and found only 12 were clearly effective, of which five were by Olweus in Scandinavia. Seven of the programmes had little effect, including one that was actually considered 'harmful'.

Taking inspiration particularly from Olweus in Scandinavia and the Sheffield project directed by Smith in England, most large projects have recommended a 'whole-school' approach. These usually share similar core features, including raising awareness of the problem, typically by devising the school's own definition of bullying and conducting pupil surveys, followed by wide consultation, staff training and the development of an anti-bullying policy.

Smith and his colleagues reviewed whole-school interventions and found that, 'Only one program [led by Olweus] yielded significant reductions in victimisation and bullying, while the other 13 yielded either negligible changes or increases on these outcomes' (Smith, Cousins & Stewart, 2005, p. 744; Smith, Schneider, Smith & Ananiadou, 2004). Unfortunately, others' attempts to independently replicate the results of the Olweus programme have proved disappointing (Olweus, 2004). Smith et al. concluded, 'The widespread enthusiasm for the whole-school approach, and its enactment into law in some jurisdictions, can be based only on the perceived urgent need to intervene and on the few studies indicating success.' They make the 'cautious recommendation' that whole-school interventions be continued, '…based not on solid evidence that the programmes work, but rather on the logical links between programs and theories about the origins of bullying and because in some instances (and under the most favourable conditions researchers have been able to contrive) they have been effective.' (their parentheses, Smith et al., 2004, p. 550, 557-558)

Some negative outcomes are often found during or after anti-bullying initiatives, even when the average figures across all the schools within a project are positive. The uncomfortable finding that there is sometimes an increase in the reported incidence of bullying is usually interpreted as a side-effect of awareness-raising. It is not clear how one can decide whether a deterioration is the result of greater awareness of an existing, previously unidentified problem, or an actual increase in bullying incidents, as Salmivalli et al. (2005, p. 484) point out, 'It is too easy to explain positive effects as being due to the intervention and negative effects (or 'no effects') being caused by students' sensitization to bully-victim problems.' It is even less clear if a subsequent reduction in reported incidence over the longer term is evidence of the effectiveness of an anti-bullying campaign, or the project's negative effect diminishing over time.

Typically, whole-school anti-bullying projects have included recommending extra resources for teachers to use when working on anti-bullying at the classroom level. In the Sheffield project, for example, they recommended theatre groups, a video and a story book, with supporting materials for classroom use. These focused on bullying scenarios and follow-up suggestions to increase pupils' awareness. Although there was some evidence of a reduction in bullying whilst the materials were being used, the effects were only short term and, 'Some project schools found that pupils who are involved in bullying others do not always respond well to these kinds of materials.' The Sheffield team concluded, 'The extent to which these approaches are successful depends on how thoroughly and purposefully they are used. Even then, on their own, they may have little effect on pupil behaviour' (DFE, 1994, p. 41, 45).

The apparent lack of commitment from school staff to engage fully with anti-bullying recommendations has been noted by researchers, although the assumption is usually made that this needs to be overcome. For example, Limber et al. (2004, p. 69) reported that when classroom meetings, 'created particular *angst* among some teachers, who expressed discomfort in engaging students in discussions about (and other activities related to) bullying,' several other professionals offered assistance to enable them to continue.

Peterson and Rigby (1999) sought students' opinions on the effectiveness of anti-bullying activities and found they were generally sceptical. As one student said, 'Well, I think no-one really wants to talk about it because that only makes it worse.'

The concern about implementation goes beyond the evaluation of individual elements within interventions. It raises the additional question of how to overcome resistance to anti-bullying projects as a whole (Rigby & Bagshaw, 2003; Salmivalli et al., 2005). When the outcomes are disappointing, researchers sometimes imply that schools should have devoted more time and commitment to it, rather than question the overall strategy (E.g. Limber, Nation, Tracy, Melton & Flerx, 2004; Hanewinkel, 2004). At the same time, it has also been recognised that even schools that produce good results during implementation may have difficulties in sustaining positive outcomes beyond it, in the longer term (Smith, Sharp, Elsea & Thompson, 2004; Galloway & Roland, 2004).

In 2006, the Office of the Children's Commissioner for England produced a report called *Bullying Today* which summarized the present position. After a thorough review of the evidence the report concluded, 'Despite the array of policies and practices described, and the promise of reductions for the future, there is actually no indication of whether bullying has been rising or falling overall.' And yet, as pointed out in the report, the suggestions still offered to schools today remain very much the same.

Following the accounts of major intervention projects from around the world, Pepler et al. (2004, p. 313) concluded that, 'At this stage in the development and refinement of bullying interventions, the research is not at the point where we can reliably point to specific elements of interventions that are known to be the active and essential elements associated with change.'

So it is timely to consider how recent ideas in facilitating change can contribute to a better understanding of how to identify more effective ways to reduce bullying in schools.

## Solution-focused practice

'Solution-focused' practice is a whole new and different way of helping people bring about improvement in their lives and in the communities or organisations to which they belong. The development of this way of working is pre-eminently associated with the Brief Family Therapy Center in Milwaukee, under the leadership of Steve de Shazer and Insoo Kim Berg (de Shazer, 1982, 1985, 1988, 1991, 1994; de Shazer et al., 2007; Berg, 1999; De Jong & Berg, 2008). They are widely acknowledged as the first to clearly articulate the solution-focused approach in individual and family therapy, starting in the late 1970s and continuing until their deaths in 2005 and 2007 respectively.

Most of us can recall a time when someone helped us or we helped someone else, maybe significantly, perhaps even in a single conversation. We may not have been aware of it at the time and in an isolated instance it could be dismissed as just a 'fluke', since we cannot know exactly which parts of any conversation were most helpful.

In their research for better and more consistent ways of resolving clients' problems, de Shazer's team observed therapeutic sessions closely to discover which specific elements of conversations proved to be the most useful. Once they had identified what worked in bringing about the change their clients wanted, they did more of it. Crucially, they complemented this by stopping doing the things that did not work so well. Their criteria for effectiveness were based on outcomes, both in terms of client satisfaction and the speed of effectiveness, judged by the number of therapy sessions given. They continually reviewed their findings, with different clients and various problems. They published their ideas and conducted ongoing research as they developed and refined their practice (De Jong & Berg, 2008).

By working in this pragmatic and disciplined way, they discovered important and surprising principles about conversations that were successful in bringing about solutions. The findings showed that their work was most effective in eliciting change when they crafted conversations in a way that helped clients concentrate on:

− Describing the preferred future
− Recognising the successful past
− Appreciating existing strengths
− Doing more of what works

Since these features are characteristic of solution-focused practice they will be returned to continually throughout this book. The implications of working in this way are far reaching.

**Describing the preferred future**

Whereas previously almost all therapy depended upon theories about problems and how therapists could help clients solve them, de Shazer and Berg found that in practice their clients' solutions had no direct or logical connection to their problems. Once this was realized, the therapist's expertise in causes and symptoms or assessment and diagnosis of any difficulties became superfluous and even seen to hinder progress. As a result, they stopped inviting their clients to talk in any depth about their problems. Instead, they found it more helpful to 'stay on the surface' (de Shazer, 1994), asking clients to describe their goal in coming to therapy and formulating questions to discover what their life would be like without the problem. Solution-focused interviewing is 'action-oriented', so in particular, clients may be asked what they will be doing differently and what others will notice them doing once they begin making progress towards their goal.

To illustrate: if a student wants help with a problem of bullying in school, rather than ask for details about the bullying, it is more helpful to ask about how exactly they want their life to be like in school in the future and what precise differences this will make. For example: *When no-one is bullying you, what difference will this make to you? What will you be doing that's different?*

Details about the problem, beyond its absence, are unnecessary to envisage this future. The aim is to get a rich description of what students want to be happening more and especially what they want to be doing differently. The more detailed and vivid this description becomes, the more it acts as a mental rehearsal for future action, so the more likely it is to happen. Put simply, it is more effective in bringing about change to concentrate attention on what is wanted, rather than what is not wanted.

**Recognising the successful past**

When clients describe what they want instead of the problem, they can usually bring to mind times when there have been exceptions to the problem or where their preferred future is already happening, even if only a little or infrequently. When someone is stuck in a problem, these occasions can remain unnoticed or be dismissed as unimportant exceptions, caused by chance or other factors outside their control.

For example, during a solution-focused interview, one student identified that he enjoyed maths, although he could not think why that might be, other than during these lessons he did not get called names. With deliberate curiosity, he was asked what exactly he was doing differently in maths. He explained that he enjoyed working in a group with other students and concentrating on getting his work done. This recognition of his successful past, in contrast to times when the problem was happening, helped increase his awareness of what was already working for at least part of the time, i.e. being with a group of other students and getting on with his lesson.

'This process of solution development can be summed up as helping an unrecognised difference become a difference that makes a difference' (de Shazer, 1988, p. 10). In solution-focused interviewing, these times of relative success are actively sought out and amplified. Recognising the successful past provides clients with the most important source of ideas that can help them become more effective at bringing about their preferred future.

**Appreciating existing strengths**
As clients talk about the times when they are more successful, their skills and strengths rather than their weaknesses come to the fore. Appreciating and complimenting clients' own strengths draws attention to what enabled them to succeed, even if only a little bit or for a brief period of time. Compliments are an important part of solution-focused therapy and appreciation is implicit throughout the interview. In subsequent sessions the smallest sign of movement towards the goal is identified and the skills and personal qualities that enabled the client to manage this progress are highlighted and complimented.

Appreciation of existing strengths is made most explicit near the end of a session when recommendations of how to move forward may be considered. In the example given above, the student might be complimented on the skills that enabled him to work well with other students in a group or helped him concentrate on his work. When the student's appropriate strengths are noticed and complimented, he is more likely to use them again. At this point, skills and strengths are the bridge (De Jong & Berg, 2008) that links the successful past with the preferred future.

### Doing more of what works

When working in a solution-focused way, tasks are not imposed on the client. Suggestions about actions the client might take, however, are often made toward the end of a session. These are intentionally small and easily manageable, usually doing more of something that has worked in the past. When suggestions are based on something the client already knows how to do successfully, progress towards the goal is likely to be quicker and more sustainable. In practice, the mere identification of a client's past achievements and existing strengths can motivate them to make progress towards their preferred future.

Taking again the example of the student who did not notice being mocked when he worked in a group, one suggestion could be that he might watch out for other lessons when he manages to work well within a group. There is a good chance that since this has already provided the conditions where he was not called names in the past, it will be effective as a deliberate strategy in the future. What is more, it is a strategy that he can probably follow immediately, since knowing it has succeeded before gives him the confidence he needs to repeat it.

In contrast, when attention is drawn to the problem and by implication to someone's weaknesses, students can often become defensive and resistant to any suggestions for change. De Shazer called resistance the clients' 'unique way of attempting to cooperate' by letting the therapist know a suggestion was not right for them at the time and that the therapist needed to try something different (de Shazer, 1994).

This is not to say that therapists never give advice. Advice in terms of information may occasionally be given but a client is the better judge of whether it is useful to them at that time. In solution-focused practice the relationship between the therapist and client has fundamentally shifted, from one where the therapist's expertise is most highly valued to one where the client's knowledge about their own lives is privileged as the more fruitful source of solutions (de Shazer, 1994). Solution-focused expertise does not lie in knowing what is best for the client and persuading the client to comply. The skill is in 'leading from behind' (De Shazer & Dolan, 2007), in asking questions that will draw attention to and amplify the client's own knowledge and experience about what is helpful.

Thus de Shazer & Berg made their therapeutic conversations 'solution-focused' as opposed to 'problem-solving'. They found the more they managed to become solution focused, the more successful they became. Indeed, once the basic principles were established, good practice became how to apply them most effectively. The approach is elegant both in its simplicity and internal integrity – they encouraged clients to reflect on what they were already managing to do that worked and to do more of it, just as they were continually doing themselves in the development of solution-focused therapy.

Independent research has begun to confirm that this approach is at least as effective as other therapies over a wide range of problems and reaches a satisfactory conclusion more quickly, sometimes in a single session and typically in three to five sessions, without sacrificing longer-term outcomes (Macdonald, 2007). In referrals specifically for bullying, solution-focused interviewing has proved similarly powerful (Young & Holdorf, 2003).

It is possible for motivated people to learn the techniques of solution-focused interviewing in just a few days, and to a skill level where they can use them and see positive results straight away. At first it may seem startling that such a powerful therapeutic approach is so apparently accessible. However, that is not to say it is easy: it requires a major change in general practice and assumptions; it can be hard for people to orientate themselves to it in the first place; and it can prove even more difficult to maintain and develop in their everyday practice. Moreover, becoming solution focused is an ever-continuing journey. Nevertheless, the absence of problem analysis and assessment makes the approach safe, adaptable and suitable for people to use beyond the therapeutic profession.

At roughly the same time as the emergence of solution-focused therapy, a management consultant named David Cooperrider was independently discovering similar principles when helping to bring about change in large organisations (Annis Hammond, 1996). Cooperrider found that concentrating on solving problems within an organisation was not as helpful as creating a vision of the organisation operating at its best, based on articulating shared values and appreciating the existing strengths and good practice. This approach in management consultancy became known as 'Appreciative Inquiry'. Although these insights into facilitating change arose in the separate fields of therapy and management consultancy, the principles they share have been recognised. Many specialists in therapy have been able to adapt their skills to professional coaching and consultancy (Furman & Ahola, 2006, 2007; Jackson & McKergow, 2002). What works on the micro-level of therapy is also effective at the macro-level of organisations.

Solution-focused work, whether at an individual or group level or within a larger organisation such as a school, is a means of helping people achieve what they want in their personal or working lives. In order to do this, inquiry is crafted in such a way that it helps clarify how someone's personal or professional life will be different when they become more like the person they want to be, or their organisation becomes more like they want it to be. Solution-focused questions help people to notice how far they have come in achieving this already and what resources they already possess to draw on to make further progress. When they are aware of what their next small sign of progress will be, they are more likely to recognise it and thereby discover how to advance even further. Solution-focused conversations are designed to help people move closer to achieving their potential.

## Solution-focused practice in schools

Some of the best-known pioneers of a solution-focused approach in school settings are Molnar & Lindquist (1989), Durrant (1995), Furman & Ahola (1992), Metcalf (1995) and Rhodes & Ajmal (1995). These authors showed with increasing detail, perceptiveness and scope, how solution-focused ideas could be applied to all kinds of problems in schools.

At first, the approach was recommended to help staff and pupils change problem behaviour. Durrant and Metcalf give examples of how solution-focused ideas can be applied to a wide range of behaviour difficulties. Furman produced a children's workbook, *Kids' Skills*, transforming misbehaviour into 'skills to be learned'. Rhodes and Ajmal extended the application to include consultation with teachers about behaviour management, help for children with reading difficulties and organisational work such as planning training for teachers.

Although the majority of solution-focused practice so far has concentrated on helping clients move closer to their preferred future, without attempting to 'solve' problems, it has nevertheless generally been described and used within the context of problems. For example, helping children with behaviour difficulties rather than improving all student behaviour, or supporting children with learning difficulties rather than coaching all pupils to improve their learning.

Once solution-focused ideas were taken beyond the bounds of problem-solving professionals such as therapists and counsellors, and into schools, education staff recognized the relevance of solution-focused ideas for developing good practice for all pupils. Solution-focused principles fit equally well within the inclusive and universal educational context where the presumption is that everyone has strengths on which to build. The school curriculum is designed on the basis of what we want children to learn and can learn, rather than on the knowledge or skills they lack. The great majority of assessment in education is designed to measure how far students have progressed so they can move onto the next step. Even where pupils are identified as having special educational needs, teaching has been moving away from diagnostic testing and remediating deficits since the late 1970s (Ainscow & Tweddle, 1979). The primary aim of schools is to help students fulfil their potential, or move closer to fulfilling it, rather than to solve their problems. At its best, education is a solution-focused endeavour, bringing about positive change in children by building on what they already know and can do, making the most of their abilities to enable them to achieve their preferred futures.

Where there are no problems to solve, and therefore no need of 'solutions', solution-focused practice might more accurately be described as 'potential-focused'. As such, it is relevant for all members of the school community, including staff, pupils, parents and supporting services, since they all have a common goal of realising children's potential. It is a model for all schools, not just for addressing problems in schools, or for schools with problems; it is a model for all pupils, not just for problems with pupils, or pupils with problems. Thus the solution-focused approach can be recognised as having a broader remit. In schools, the possibilities have only just begun for using solution-focused practice to improve professional development, teaching and learning, academic attainment, partnership with parents, extra-curricular achievements, attendance and behaviour – in fact anywhere there is a desire to maximise potential.

The principles that de Shazer discovered were of a higher order than simply finding solutions to problems. Anyone who wants to promote positive change to fulfil the potential of an individual or organisation, or to help someone 'do justice to themselves and their own beliefs in a way that gives them pride' (George, Iveson & Ratner, 1999, p. 28) will welcome de Shazer's insights into how best to help bring about change.

Solution-focused practice is the means by which goals can be achieved without any need to go searching for problems to solve, or barriers to overcome, and regardless of whether there is a problem or not.

### An anti-bullying day in a secondary school

I was approached by a year coordinator in a secondary school who had agreed, on reflection she thought rather hastily, to organise an anti-bullying day for her year group. Having heard that I had been doing anti-bullying work in schools, she hoped I could help. With the day fast approaching, the teacher was worried she had no ideas what to do.

I suggested that rather than her taking responsibility for coming up with the activities, the teachers involved could use their own existing expertise. I mentioned that I had tried to commission a dancer to help in my project, to which she replied, 'Of course! I'm a dance specialist – that would be no problem for me.' The theme was anti-bullying with the accent on promoting friendship and cooperation. The only constraint on the teachers was that a discrete piece of work needed to be completed for display or performance by the end of the day.

All the students gathered in the gym (the largest space available) for the last hour of the day when each had a short time to show everyone else the work they had produced. The sports department kicked off by demonstrating collaborative team-building games and their two groups competed to manhandle a bench up, over and around an obstacle course. They also managed to clear the equipment away in double-quick time. Some students recited the poetry and free writing they had composed in the English department. The drama group demonstrated collaborative activities including 'hot-seating'. The art students displayed posters they had designed. Other students performed raps they had composed with the help of staff from the music department, and the year coordinator's group performed their dance.

The students clearly enjoyed the challenge and showed their enthusiastic appreciation for the work the other groups had done. The teachers were equally pleased. The head of the sports department thought the students had derived so much from the team-building activities that he would consider including them more often in the curriculum. The headteacher came to watch the performances and was clearly moved and delighted with the success of the day.

## A solution-focused perspective on anti-bullying programmes

The main principles of solution-focused work can predict activities likely to be successful and differentiate them from strategies that are unhelpful or may even be harmful. This applies both to specific elements within programmes and to overall project management, for 'no matter how good a solution might seem, if it does not work it is not a solution' (De Shazer & Dolan, 2007, p. 2).

### Describing the preferred future

The main assumption underpinning most anti-bullying work so far – expert knowledge about the problem of bullying can help schools to reduce it – implies that on a scale of 1 to 10, where 1 is *the worst that bullying could be in a school,* 10 would be *no bullying.*

In contrast, just as De Shazer found it more helpful to work on clients' own positive goals and encourage them to describe their future without the problem, solution-focused anti-bullying redirects concentration towards a description of what schools want to be happening when relationships between pupils fulfil their positive potential. On a solution–focused scale of 1 to 10, where 1 is *the worst bullying could be in a school,* 10 would not merely be the absence of bullying, but rather the presence of *a safe, friendly and supportive environment.* Solution-focused practice facilitates and 'thickens' a school's description of the preferred future, since the more detailed and familiar this description is and the more it is rehearsed, the more likely it is to happen.

Teachers know that giving attention, even negative attention, to any particular behaviour tends to reinforce it. It seems at least feasible that drawing attention to bullying might be a self-defeating strategy. Raising awareness runs the risk of increasing rather than reducing bullying because it focuses attention on the behaviour we want to stop. That unacceptable risk can be avoided by concentrating on raising awareness of what is wanted instead: the preferred future. This is not to ignore the issue of bullying but to address it in the most effective way possible.

## Recognising the successful past

Another characteristic of solution-focused practice is the identification of existing success. The phenomenon of not realising the significance of what was already working was noticed by de Shazer. At first, when they began working with a client they made the assumption that the therapist had to initiate change (1988, p. xv). As they developed their practice, they realized that this was untrue and that in fact clients were already doing something that worked before they came to therapy. This insight became fundamental to helping people discover ways of bringing about further improvement: There are always exceptions to the problem. There are always times when the problem is not happening, or is happening less.

Since anti-bullying programmes have generally been thought of as initiating change in schools, the significance of existing good practice has generally gone unrecognised. Mellor (1999) is unusual in drawing attention to the wide and unexplained variations in the level of bullying between schools. In his sample survey in ten secondary schools in Scotland, where varying levels of bullying could not be attributed to other factors such as size of school or pupil intake, the rates of children who reported being bullied in individual schools ranged from 2.4% to 15.4%. Incidentally, none of these schools had an anti-bullying policy. Stevens et al. (2004) found a similar wide difference in their sample from 84 Flemish schools, where levels of bullied pupils varied from 8.5% to 46% in primary schools and from 5% to 29% in secondary schools.

A solution-focused perspective on these surveys would suggest that some schools are already dealing very effectively with bullying. A solution-focused approach is curious about relative success because it is evidence for the presence of effective practice.

Pupil questionnaires contain more evidence of schools' successful work. It has been estimated from the responses prior to any intervention that the incidence of pupils being bullied reduces as they get older by about 15% per year (DFE, 1994; Smith et al., 1999; Olweus, 2004). Understandably, researchers seek ways of eliminating this 'natural' reduction in bullying in order to measure the 'value-added' effect of their programmes. Bearing in mind this average yearly reduction is greater than achieved by most published anti-bullying programmes, and in the absence of evidence to the contrary, solution-focused practitioners would assume that schools contribute to this reduction and would be asking: *What are school staff doing already that helps reduce pupils' susceptibility to bullying as they get older?* This, and other similar questions, helps to identify what works.

Importantly, since solution-focused practice works independently of any theories about problems, solution-focused questions have the potential to be helpful regardless of the validity of any prevailing assumptions. (In fact, the idea that bullying reduces year on year has been challenged [Salmivalli, 2002]). As most theories about bullying and how to reduce it may be subject to contradictory evidence and change over time and cultural context, independence from theory is an invaluable strength of a solution-focused approach. Whether the theory is right or wrong, the acid test of effectiveness is outcome – does it work? For the assumptions behind any enquiry to be helpful, they only need to be both credible at that particular time and place, and sensitive to any signs of success.

Recognising pre-existing good practice provides clues to more straightforward solutions. The sure way to identify effective anti-bullying activity is to search for evidence of it happening in schools. Once recognised, doing more of it is likely to lead to further reductions in bullying.

## Appreciating existing strengths

Solution-focused practitioners actively seek and appreciate existing strengths, realising their significance in making progress. As Ajmal writes, 'People do not change by drawing on their deficits, they use their resources' (2001, p. 27). Similarly, Galloway & Roland (2004, p. 41-42) point out, 'the word "development" in professional development implies the importance of building on existing practice with an existing knowledge base. The core tasks of teaching are to create a social climate which pupils value and in which they want to learn, and to create an educational climate which enhances pupils' learning.' A successful anti-bullying project is built on teachers' professional knowledge and resourcefulness in promoting a positive social ethos.

By their very nature, the answers to questions about the skills schools possess, drawn from the evidence of their successes, will be as individual as the personnel at each school and the community it serves. The activities that promote good peer relationships in any school can be remarkably diverse because they also contribute to the wider curriculum. Clubs, field trips, sports, music and drama performances and a host of other activities can all contribute to the social cohesion and ethos of a school. For this reason, it is difficult to create a common package of recommendations that all schools should adopt. Attempts to do this contribute to the variability of outcomes in different schools, even within the same initiative.

When schools deteriorate on key indicators in anti-bullying projects it is evidence that in those schools the pre-existing skills and practice were more effective than the changes that were introduced. Although certainly there may be general ideas about good school practice that are commonly accepted, the details about strengths and skills can be so widely varied that they can only be recognised by appreciative inquiry in individual schools.

## Doing more of what works

Solution-focused practice suggests that the smallest steps and the lightest touch that are the most effective at bringing about change. What is more, suggestions are best when they recommend doing more of what is working already. In other words, a solution-focused anti-bullying initiative takes what is already a feature of the school's success in reducing bullying, and by appreciating it energises staff to develop it further. Basing any intervention on what schools are already managing to do, extending their good practice by using their existing skills even more, is also the most sustainable way of working.

There is evidence from anti-bullying research that supports the idea that self-reliant projects are more effective. In an interesting and careful study, Stevens, Van Oost & De Bourdeaudhuij (2004) showed that when primary and secondary schools implemented their own anti-bullying programmes, they had better outcomes than schools with outside training and support. Similarly in the Sheffield project, two of the three comparison secondary schools had better key outcomes with their own anti-bullying programmes than most of the schools within the project (Whitney, Rivers, Smith & Sharp, 1994).

A solution-focused perspective suggests that the success of anti-bullying initiatives depends on how far they can tap into the existing skills and strengths available at any particular school at any particular time. When projects build on the knowledge and understanding that teachers have of day-to-day life in their own schools they are more likely to be effective and sustainable.

A solution-focused approach to reducing bullying concentrates on the preferred future of a safe, friendly and supportive school and works with the school's existing resources. Such an approach was adopted in the town of Kempele, Finland, and monitored over an extended period from 1990-98 (Koivisto, 2004). This project paid particular attention to school climate, making it more open, respectful and encouraging, in cooperation with the parents and with pupil involvement. They actively sought feedback from the pupils about what was most effective so they could do more of what worked. The project continued a system of peer support that was already highly valued. Although several training events were arranged for teachers they were given no detailed advice. The programme lasted a year but follow-up surveys continued at two-year intervals which showed that although the campaign was relatively short, the improvement was sustained. Being bullied and bullying others decreased substantially by the first follow-up and remained at more or less the same level throughout the remaining six years of monitoring.

Solution-focused anti-bullying demands a lower level of input because it deliberately moves schools in the direction that the staff identify they want to go and in the way they want to do it. More traditional, high-profile anti-bullying projects require a high degree of effort over a long period. In the absence of a corresponding improvement and with concern about the possible negative effects, staff may withdraw their commitment. Resistance in schools is the useful sign that it needs to be done differently.

In an influential article on school improvement, Hargreaves (2001) noted that, 'Teachers often put considerable effort into making changes with relatively little impact on students, so teachers become frustrated and exhausted.' The challenge is not how to persuade teachers to commit themselves to high-input interventions, but how to identify the lowest level of input that leads to the best outcomes, or as Hargreaves put it, how to 'work smarter, not harder'. A recent annual report from Ofsted emphasised just this:

> A key message from this Annual Report is that good leaders know how to assess the support offered; they take what is essential, and they resist all but the right support at the right time. This point is worth emphasising: unless external support is carefully matched to individual circumstances and its impact is rigorously evaluated, it can create more problems and, at worst, slow the pace of improvement. (2008, p. 8)

The success of schools lies along a continuum. Some schools have very low levels of bullying and only need to recognise what they already manage to do well, in order to ensure their good practice continues. Other schools will need to identify exactly where their strengths lie in order to do more of what works. The fewer the existing strengths a school has available, the more essential it becomes to identify and capitalise on them. Solution-focused work ensures the purpose of professional development is appropriate for each school. When approached in a solution-focused way, anti-bullying is a dynamic and rewarding area of positive activity that validates whatever the existing skills are in a school and uses them as resources to reach its greater potential.

## Anti-bullying in a Primary School

Following the amalgamation of two adjacent, inner-city primary schools, a group of parents complained to the local press about bullying which they believed was widespread at the new school. They organised a petition to be presented at the forthcoming Annual Governors' Meeting.

The aggrieved parents were given an invitation to visit the school before the Governors' Meeting. It was agreed that all parents should be encouraged to get involved and work with the staff to develop an effective anti-bullying policy and support their children in school.

The resulting *Parents' Anti-bullying Working Party* included all parents who volunteered, pupils from the school council, the deputy headteacher and two local authority support staff (Gail Holdorf, the anti-bullying coordinator, and myself). The working party drafted a very short anti-bullying policy, including several ideas for development that were suggested by different people at the first meeting. Regular newsletters were circulated to all parents, together with an ongoing invitation to join the working party.

By the end of term, the draft anti-bullying policy had been sent to all parents, considered by the pupil council and was ready to go for approval to governors. As the parents had suggested, a fortnightly drop-in was taking place to enable parents to see the local authority anti-bullying coordinator if they wished to talk to someone independent of the school. The deputy head was establishing a playground 'buddies' scheme, just as she had organised in her previous school. A 'Help Box' had been provided for children to request support for any problem they might have, including bullying, and a short training session was provided for classroom assistants in leading support groups for children who felt bullied.

Six months later, the working party had changed its name to the *Pupil Support Forum*. The pupils' school council reported the buddy scheme had been successful and there was also a 'friendship stop' in the playground. No parents had found it necessary to use the drop-in. Children who had taken part in support groups were interviewed on video to record their perspectives, which were entirely positive. Reviewing the records, complaints of bullying had dropped steadily from more than one a week to just one in the previous month.

One year later, the school surveyed all their children, not specifically on bullying, but on whether children were happy in school, including having friends and feeling safe. Advisers from another city came to observe the school's anti-bullying practice and subsequently incorporated it into their own authority policy. Two children were invited to represent the school at a solution-focused conference in Poland, where they answered questions most engagingly about their experience of being in support groups, illustrated by the children's video. (See further in Chapter 5)

Throughout this time of development the focus of the working party was kept firmly on the preferred future of a happy and supportive school and the small but significant steps that were being taken to get there, capitalising on the skills and strengths already available to the school. Within a year the school had shifted its reputation, from one struggling against widespread bullying to being an example of outstanding good practice.

(Thanks to Cathy Byrne, The Parks Primary School, Hull, for permission for this case study to be included)

## Summary

Management of change, whether for individuals or organisations such as schools, has so far overwhelmingly used a problem-solving model. Problem-solving and change management have become so closely associated it is sometimes assumed they are the same thing. Solution-focused thinking provides us with a new paradigm for change management that is creative, powerful and fast-acting. At a small group or individual level its discovery originated in 'solution-focused brief therapy' and at a large group or organisational level, it has been called 'appreciative inquiry'.

Regardless of whether a problem exists, when helping to bring about change for individuals or organisations, the principles of solution-focused practice are the same – helping people to notice what works and doing more of it. Effective interventions can be recognised by their focus on:
- Describing the preferred future
- Recognising the successful past
- Appreciating existing strengths

- Doing more of what works

Solution-focused practice offers schools a more effective means to reduce bullying by focusing on their preferred future. The best way of ensuring that anti-bullying does not inadvertently increase the problem is to deliberately concentrate on how schools want their community to be. Whilst concern is focused on the problem of bullying and trying to stop it, attention is diverted from fulfilling the potential to create friendly and supportive school communities. Schools do not have to presume they have 'a problem with bullying' that needs to be solved. By appreciating how anti-bullying is an integral part of teachers' work already and concentrating on the strengths they have available, schools can be more effective by continually developing an ever more friendly, safe and supportive ethos in their own unique context. This book sets out to describe how schools can promote friendship and mutually supportive relationships through solution-focused conversations at a whole-school, classroom and individual level of working.

# Chapter 2
# Professional Development

## Introduction

In Chapter 1 it was proposed that solution-focused principles could be used to differentiate effective anti-bullying strategies from those that are not so helpful or that may even be harmful. This chapter describes how features of solution-focused practice can be used in professional development for group training or individual coaching where the aim is to develop a friendly, safe and supportive school culture. A similar approach is also applied to two specific areas that schools have identified as important in promoting an anti-bullying ethos: adults acting as good role models and promoting pupils' resilience. Although both solution-focused therapists and management consultants simply engage clients in a certain kind of discourse, these conversations have been shown to be surprisingly powerful. Even though this approach is low profile, it is ultimately most effective and influences the wider culture of the school positively in addition to reducing bullying.

## Solution-focused whole-school development

In larger schools, a small steering group is often given responsibility for anti-bullying training and activities. At a whole-school level helpful conversations can be arranged between the entire staff in a training session, at times working in small groups or pairs, or within groups appropriate to the school organisation. Time can be set aside, for example, during governors' meetings, staff meetings, departmental meetings, circle-time in classes, school council meetings or parents' days.

## Describing the preferred future

In order that action to reduce bullying can become focused on the preferred future, members of the school community need to feel comfortable exploring and articulating their aspirations for the school operating at its best, when bullying is not an issue. Vision has sometimes been considered the prerogative of the headteacher or the leadership team, but all members of the school community – governors, staff, pupils and parents – have their own ideas of how they want their school to be. These tend to remain rather vague if they are not invited to articulate them very often. In a solution-focused school more time and opportunity is given to describing the potential that exists than any weaknesses or problems the school may suffer.

Leadership consists not so much in defining the vision but enabling a discussion and discovery of the shared, preferred future, together with the aims and values that implicitly underpin it. Although describing the potential of the school community might seem like a preliminary step before taking action, this is not the case. Solution-focused leaders invite staff, parents and pupils to contribute to this description on a continuing basis, knowing it is helpful in actually bringing it about – and the more vivid the detail, the more likely it is to happen.

Some well tried and tested solution-focused conversational techniques are highly adaptable for this purpose. Solution-focused scaling can be used to enable people to articulate their aspirations in a broad area of policy and to 'drill down' to identify small but significant steps. The parameters, the 1 and the 10, are defined in such a way that the present position can be construed as higher than a 1, but lower than a 10. Ideally, the scale is most useful when it is devised so the present position falls somewhere in the middle. This gives the maximum scope for appreciating both existing strengths and future possibilities. When scaling is used as a group activity, it is helpful if participants can be encouraged to come to a working consensus, without there being any suggestion that any individual's scaling is 'too high' or 'too low', since people's different perspectives and priorities will affect their view of the place on the scale.

Most solution-focused work begins with a brief orientation towards competencies rather than problems. This should only take a few minutes, before 'getting down to business'. In a training context, an appropriate short 'warm-up' exercise could involve people working with a partner to ask:

*What do staff at this school do well?*

or

*What's gone well for you today?*

or

*What have you noticed another member of staff doing well this week?*

The following is an example of using a scaling question to help describe the preferred future:

*On a scale of 1 to 10 … where 1 is 'a school that does nothing to promote friendship or mutual support' … and 10 is 'a school that is as friendly, safe and supportive as it could possibly be' …*

| 1 | 10 |
|---|---|
| Does nothing | Friendly, safe and supportive |

*Imagine you visit a school that is the best it could be (given all the constraints of resources, staffing, buildings, intake etc.) in terms of a safe, supportive and friendly community, a 10 …*
*What is the first thing you will notice about the school that tells you this?*
*What else? What next?*

These questions are not easy to answer. The manner in which the questions are asked is important. To help people to feel comfortable enough to elaborate on their ideas, the questions need to be posed in a curious rather than interrogatory way and yet with persistence. Many solution-focused questions are so open that just one single answer is not enough. The practitioners at BRIEF in London are acknowledged (de Shazer & Dolan 2008, p. 72) to have recognized the importance of *What else?* type questions.

Typical first answers might include: *staff relationships with students, the quality of the environment and facilities, relationships with parents, motivated staff, etc.*

In any solution-focused conversation the most useful, action-oriented answers are rarely voiced at the outset, so it is important to keep asking for more and more specific details, to ensure the answers reveal the most helpful ideas.

*What would we see that tells us staff have good relationships with pupils?*

The aim is to continue to elicit more details, the 'small differences that make all the difference', such as *students smile and say 'hello', reception staff are welcoming, senior staff are there to greet parents, visitors are offered a drink …*

After sharing ideas, a useful extension of this line of enquiry is to consider the lists in terms of what they demonstrate about the values everyone wants to promote in school. Ideas can be grouped together under three or four main headings (Annis Hammond, 1996). For example, several may be placed under the heading of 'a friendly place to be', or 'everyone in the community is valued' or 'we want the school to feel safe' etc. As a result, a short list of aims and aspirations can be highlighted that underpin any policy or practice the school wants to develop. Values are implicit in the details of the vision of what the school community wants to happen – and they will inevitably encompass anti-bullying values such as respect for others and their differences.

## Friendship Week

Mention has been made of the government's plan that all schools in England should have an anti-bullying week in the autumn term each year. Some schools have decided instead to call it 'friendship week', or something similar, since this emphasizes what they wish to promote rather than what they are trying to reduce. Activities to promote friendship are also more enjoyable, for staff as well as pupils.

The change of title is not merely cosmetic. When teachers are asked to put forward ideas, suggestions for an anti-bullying week are quite different from those for a friendship week. Solution-focused principles would indicate that proposals for a friendship week are likely to be more effective in reducing bullying, since they draw attention to the preferred future.

## Recognising the successful past

Using the scaling again, the following questions amplify existing good practice:

> Given that 1 is 'this school does nothing', and 10 is 'the best this school could be in terms of a safe, supportive and friendly community' (given all the constraints of resources, staffing, buildings, intake, etc.) where is this school right now?

| 1 | 7? | 10 |
|---|---|---|
| Does nothing | | Friendly, safe and supportive |

Once there is a roughly agreed consensus, the very next questions will be:

> What makes it so high? What else?
> What are we doing already that makes it a 6 and not a 5? [Or an 8 and not a 7? Or even, a 2 and not a 1?]

When morale is high, staff have no difficulty in describing their good practice – they are proud of what they have already achieved and are happy to talk about it. The areas identified may include themes in the curriculum, peer support schemes, pastoral arrangements, assembly topics, merit systems, special events or visiting speakers, etc.

When confidence is not so high, any contributions to a supportive environment can seem to be 'exceptions' or flukes, and can easily go unnoticed or be disregarded as unimportant. The conversation can easily turn into a discussion about why the point on the scale is not higher, in other words, the talk becomes about problems.

In solution-focused work, when the successful past is exceptional, it is particularly valued and explored for signs of a possible way forward. In one school where there were difficulties with pupils' behaviour, the only positive area initially identified was staff working as a team.

Follow-up questions amplified specific details of how teamwork helped:

> *How does teamwork show itself?*
> *How do staff know they have the support of the team?*
> *How does the leadership team promote teamwork?*

The staff identified: *Working together to ensure pupils were calm entering the school; sharing ideas and resources; helping if someone is having difficulties with a pupil; watching out for each others' classes ...*

The more these areas of effectiveness can be elaborated, the more they will be reinforced and made stronger. There is no need to explore any weaknesses there might be. Improvement can be reached more easily by building on what staff already do well. Identifying weaknesses, threats and barriers is a problem-oriented, morale-sapping endeavour. 'If an organisation keeps hearing how ill it is and how much it has to fix itself, members will behave as if the organisation were ill' (S Annis Hammond, 1996, p. 26). In fact, because what we focus on tends to grow, the recognition of even small successes will help to move the school in the direction that is wanted, without doing anything further.

## Appreciating existing strengths

It is helpful if existing strengths are explicitly appreciated. Listening out specifically for skills and positive qualities, to practise what Eve Lipchik called 'listening with a constructive ear' (George, Iveson & Ratner, 1990, p. 38) is encouraged by knowing beforehand that positive feedback will be given. When staff have their strengths recognized, they can be motivated to do more of what works. The simplest compliment begins with:

> *I am impressed by ...*

Followed by details from the previous conversation:

> *... the organisation of the peer support scheme.*
> *... the way the team works together.*

Compliments and appreciation form a 'bridge' from the past to the preferred future.

## Help box

Occasionally a student may be grateful for a means to summon help in confidence and some schools provide a 'bully box' for students to report bullying. This might give the impression, perhaps mistakenly, that there is a problem with bullying. On the other hand, a 'help box' draws attention to the caring and supportive qualities of school staff, whatever the issue.

## Doing more of what works

Solution-focused schools identify small but significant steps that build on evidence of what has worked in the past to move immediately towards the preferred future. They work 'smarter, not harder'. It is easier, quicker and more respectful of the substantial efforts staff put into their work to build on existing success rather than start from scratch. Indeed, if existing good practice has not been appreciated, any future proposals are more likely to fail. Practical suggestions follow quite naturally once the present strengths and skills that will make further development possible have been overtly complimented.

Scaling can be used to identify specific areas for development. For example, if the consensus about the present position were a 6:

| 1 | 6 | 7 | 10 |
|---|---|---|---|
| Does nothing | | | Friendly, safe and supportive |

*So, given we are about a 6 now, how will we know when we are a 7?*
*What will we be doing that's different?*
*What difference will that make to us/you?*
*What will the students be doing differently when it is a 7?*
*What will parents notice?*

The questions begin, *How will we know when we are a 7?* This is not the same as *How do we get to a 7?* The latter question somehow implies change is difficult whereas solution-focused questions tend to assume change is inevitable. Any suggestions generated by these questions will be informed by existing knowledge and good practice, the skills already available and related possibilities. One place further along the scale is manageable yet significant progress.

If the school has identified, for example, that one way a caring ethos has been promoted is by encouraging older students to support younger ones, this good practice might be extended, say, to mentoring pupils in their transition to secondary school. As such, the action is not remedial; it is not necessarily about solving a problem. It is about appreciating new possibilities that extend from existing experience.

The school that identified its strength was working as a team, decided to work on improving how pupils moved along the corridors and into the assembly hall. One of the advantages of using scaling is that any ideas will fit with the present level of effectiveness and capacity for change.

By planning in this way, schools capitalise on any resources available to them either within or outside the school. It is innovative and unique to that school's own situation and grounded in its own experience, so everyone can be confident that it will work. Of course, there can be no guarantees. Other priorities can emerge in time, or things may occur beyond anyone's control to throw any action off course. Nonetheless, acting on the basis of existing strengths gives the best possible chance of success in the future. Two or three ideas can be prioritised for action in the immediate future, i.e. tomorrow, next week, this half term. For example, someone may volunteer to ask their class for ideas about supporting new pupils who are joining the school.

### Lunchtime supervisor training

This is an example of two sessions of training with lunchtime supervisors in a primary school identified as in need of support for behaviour. The main questions are shown in italics and the supervisors' responses are shown as bullet points. Their suggestions, in their own words, were written up on a flip-chart at the time.

I planned to begin the first session by asking what they enjoyed about their work. Someone commented that lunchtimes were 'not as bad as they had been'. Too good an opportunity to miss, I invited them to say how lunchtimes had been improving recently. They said there was now more equipment for the children to play with.

*So what difference does having more equipment make?*
- Less fighting
- Something the children look forward to

- Children are not bored
- They mix more and share better
- The atmosphere is better

   *What tells you the atmosphere is better?*
- Children are more settled
- Not so much 'cheekiness' from pupils *[So what are children saying now, instead?]*
- Children ask the supervisors to join in games
- The supervisors have gained more respect and trust
- They are talking more to children
- Children are talking more to them
- Children are talking more, relationships improving, particularly with naughty kids

Since 'talking' was mentioned several times and therefore identified by them as important …
   *How have you managed to get the children to talk more?*
- The supervisors were finding things to praise
- Giving children jobs
- Realising the children need attention
- Offering to help them
- The supervisors feel more included

It is not obvious how feeling more included would lead to the children to talk more. Therefore it was probably worth inquiring further about this, since the supervisors recognized it contributed to managing the children better.
   *So what has happened to help them feel more included?*
- They are told clearly what is expected of them
- They are kept informed about what is going on in school
- Meetings concerning their work are arranged for them
- Their views heard and taken account of
- They know where they stand
- Shouting has improved a lot already and being outside with the children

Any area where improvement is already identified is worth exploring...
> *Shouting has improved a lot already. So what are you doing now, instead?*

- Count to 10
- Smile and walk away
- Give a stern look
- Make a joke
- Be extra polite
- Don't argue with them

> *So, on a scale of 1 to 10, where 1 is 'shouting all the time' and 10 is 'nobody shouts at all', where are you now?*

They agreed they were already about a 5.

> *So, given the progress you have made already, if I come back in two weeks' time, will it be even better?*

In two weeks they thought it would be a 7. We arranged a review in two weeks' time to see how they got on, and how they managed to do it. In the second session, after a quick summary of the last meeting, they wanted to tell me that they all thought they were now an 8 and seemed very pleased with how they had worked together to achieve it.

> *That's fantastic! After all, you were only thinking it might be a 7! How did you manage to get to an 8?*

- The supervisors all made a determined effort
- They were all in agreement
- Children are more involved in playing
- The organisation of games has improved
- More kids are joining in the games
- Children get a say in what's happening the next day
- Difficult children are now having more fun
- Having more laughs with the children
- Happier environment all round
- There is not the need to shout any more
- They deliberately divert children from trouble

They were complimented on what they had managed to achieve and how their attitude and commitment to working as a team suggested they would be able to continue to make lunchtimes better in the future. There was a discussion about what they would expect to notice improving next. They suggested being out in the playground promptly with the children. They were already actively considering organisational changes to allow that to happen.

During staff development or planning in a steering group, the ideas can be gathered together and an action plan written up, for whenever evidence is required. I call these 'live action plans' because they are a far cry from the rather dry, time consuming, lengthy documents that get put away in a folder to be brought out for review at some later date, sometimes with vague apprehension.

In practical terms, during larger training activities, it is helpful to ask people to work together in small groups that fit with the organisation of the school. Each group can prioritise two or three ideas at each stage and write them on self-sticking notes. They can be placed into the appropriate column of a skeleton action plan on a large chart which can be typed up later, if necessary, although leaving it in sticky note form means it can easily be updated and the plan stays 'live' in real time. By action planning in this way, everyone involved can see their contribution, based on their shared vision and ideas for progress, using their existing strengths. After suggestions are put into practice they can be moved across to the 'successful past' or 'strengths' column. One school used this format very effectively to produce and monitor the post-inspection action plan displayed in their staff room. Appendix A gives a simple example to illustrate this kind of planning. It charts how possible actions for the future build on ideas previously mentioned, as the discussion moves across the columns of an action plan from left to right.

It only remains to ensure that even the smallest steps towards success are recognized and appreciated, and indeed celebrated when appropriate. It is too easy to concentrate on solving problems, moving from one issue to the next, thinking progress is being made when in fact the school may just be managing to be 'satisfactory'. Celebration of success is not just a pleasant optional extra; in a solution-focused school it is used to validate the direction of travel and encourage a continuing commitment to it.

### Focusing on identified priorities

Actions identified during solution-focused conversations are unique to each school's preferred future and closely related to the school's present level of effectiveness and existing good practice. As the possibilities for action towards improvement diverge and multiply, it becomes increasingly difficult to specify what further action or aspects of professional development would be most useful. Indeed, any package of recommended strategies may unintentionally replace superior practice already in place. To demonstrate how priorities can be further explored, those elements mentioned frequently by headteachers and other staff as being significant in providing a friendly and supportive school, have been used as examples. These include adults acting as good role models, and promoting resilience and self-esteem.

## Adults acting as role models

In schools where a strong supportive ethos exists between pupils, the single feature mentioned most commonly by staff is that adults act as good role models. Adult behaviour provides a powerful example in school which pupils unconsciously imitate. Most staff are aware of their influence and appreciate the responsibility this places on them to act in a way that conforms to the aims and values the school wishes to promote.

A common understanding of bullying is that it is a means of achieving or maintaining power or status. If so, it is not surprising that we may be tempted to respond in a bullying manner when our power or status in various roles as adults is threatened. At one time, bullying of pupils by teachers was routine. Corporal punishment, humiliation, shouting and threatening were thought to be acceptable, even commendable strategies to maintain discipline. The rejection of bullying as a legitimate strategy for teachers, and indeed all staff in school, has meant that nowadays staff actively undermine bullying patterns of behaviour, for example by modelling calm self-control under provocation and a respectful and understanding attitude to others. Although most of us would admit that under pressure we are liable to fall somewhat short of perfection, the majority of school staff recognizes these features of good practice when they are working at their best.

During staff development it is more effective to help staff articulate their own potential, how they *want* to be, than to urge them however delicately toward what they *ought* to be. Focusing on what staff do when they are at their best and enabling this to be articulated in detail, encourages more of it. If a school wants to improve, or simply reinforce and celebrate the models that staff project to pupils in school, then the following coaching conversations can be useful. These examples can be deployed in a training session with staff working in pairs:

> *When you are at your best in the classroom, how do you recognize this?*
> *What do you do, exactly?*
> *How does this help students?*
> *What difference does this make to you?*
> *What does your closest colleague notice about you when you are at your best?*

Or

> *If you accidentally overheard something a student said about you, what would you be most pleased to hear?*
> *If your line manager wrote a reference for you, what aspects of your relationships with students would you most like to see included?*

Inquiring about specific occasions when people have been at their best when under pressure encourages yet more detail about successful practice:

> *Think of a time recently when you handled a difficult situation with a student, so that it preserved a good working relationship.*
> *What exactly did you do well?*
> *What did the student notice about how you dealt with the difficulty?*
> *What did other pupils notice?*

Interviewees' strengths can be highlighted by further questions, such as:

> *What were you most pleased to notice about yourself?*
> *What made you think of handling a difficult situation in this way?*

Or, it can be done with straightforward compliments:
*I noticed how well you managed to ...*
*I'm impressed by how you handled that difficult situation by ...*

Encouraging more of what works:
*If there was one aspect of your relationships with pupils you have*
*mentioned that you would like to be even better, what would it be?*
*When that happens, what will be different about you?*
*Who else will notice this first?*
*What will the students notice about you?*
*What will your closest colleague notice that's different?*
*How will this benefit you?*

Solution-focused conversations such as these are very powerful in validating best practice. They enable teachers and other staff to become more like the role-models they wish to be for students, by reinforcing and extending the skills and strengths they already use in their relationships.

## Coaching an individual teacher
The same solution-focused strategies can be used when a member of staff has a problem, although the interviewer will need to listen even more carefully to identify instances when the difficulties appear less troublesome. Scaling is particularly useful when this is the case.

A teacher was referred by the school head because he was having difficulties managing behaviour in class. In the first session, he admitted being shocked by the way students spoke to him. He had attended a school where students would never have dared to answer back as they did at this school. He found this made him very angry and he supposed that did not help, since his shouting made no difference at all.

He was asked what would be different, when the students were being just a little more respectful. He said that he would not feel so bad at the end of the day and dread coming to school the next. On a scale of 1 to 10, where 1 is *the worst it could get and he had decided he was not coming into school again*, and 10 was *feeling okay at the end of the day*, where would he say it was now? He thought it was at about 4.

Asked what made it a 4 and not a 3 or even lower, he replied a few of his lessons were 'not that bad'. The conversation subsequently focused on these lessons. He found that generally the class behaved better when students listenened without interrupting too much while he was explaining at the beginning what they had to do. Describing in detail one lesson that was 'fairly okay', he said he had sat on a chair while he talked to them, which was unusual. I asked what was different about him when he was sitting down to talk. He said he felt more relaxed and the students seemed to be paying more attention, 'It was quite good actually, I felt like I'd got somewhere at last'. The students were calmer and talking more sensibly. He was asked for more and more detail about how sitting down had helped – his posture and tone of voice, how he replied to students' comments and what exactly the students did that made him feel he had 'got somewhere' with them. Another lesson that proved satisfactory was one where he had made sure beforehand that all the equipment he needed was ready in the classroom – something not always easy to manage, but a classroom assistant had offered to help on that occasion.

After discussing what was different about him during lessons that had been a little better, and what he could remember of these lessons, the teacher was asked what would be different when he was 6 on the scale. He said he would be making sure in the evening that he knew what he would be doing in his lessons the next day. At the moment he was so worried, he avoided thinking about it and this probably added to his pre-class anxieties. In the past he had previewed his lessons the evening before, but had begun to feel it was just not worth it.

The teacher was complimented for his openness and determination to keep trying, despite the difficulties. I suggested he watch out for the occasions when it was a 6 or more in class and we would review what he noticed about these times in the following session.

The next session he appeared more optimistic. He said there had been one 'horrendous' day, but otherwise it had been quite a good week. He put himself at about a 7 on the scale. When asked what was different now, he said he had decided to stay more at the front of the class. When a student needed help, he asked them to come to him so he could still keep an eye on the rest of the class. As a result he had definitely felt more comfortable. After a further session, he said he had begun to 'get a bit more organised' and been able to meet up with friends for an evening out. He had gone up to 8 on the scale and although teaching was 'certainly not easy', he was no longer dreading coming into school and was managing to have a joke with other younger members of staff who also found some of the children difficult.

The teacher had expected initially that I would want to observe one of his worst lessons and admitted he was worried about what I might say or what might be reported back to the headteacher. It is normal practice to give support for behaviour by observing a lesson to identify weaknesses and offer advice about how to put them right. I have done this in the past myself but nowadays if I observe a class I find it more helpful to identify what the teacher does well and encourage them to do more of what appears to work.

## Promoting self-esteem and resilience

Another factor that teachers believe is important in developing an ethos where everyone is valued, is to nurture pupils' self-esteem. Daniel Goleman's book *Emotional Intelligence* (1996) has been influential in arguing that schools have an important role to play in promoting good mental health. It has been estimated that about 2% of primary age children, rising to 5% of secondary age children, might be seriously depressed (UK Office for National Statistics, 2004).

Social support from family, peers and school staff is an important factor in protecting children from psychological distress. Most children are resilient enough to weather the emotional ups and downs life brings them, including temporary unhappiness or anxiety at home or in school (See Craig, 2009). Since schools realise the importance of social support and resilience, they find many ways to encourage a healthy self-confidence. They celebrate student successes and encourage pupils to take responsibility for themselves and others. Teachers invite pupils to participate in decisions that affect them, from nursery children making simple choices from a variety of activities, to older students being electing representatives for a school council and contributing to the interviewing of new staff.

Teachers are often concerned about students who show signs of low self-esteem and this has often been associated with being bullied or vulnerability to bullying. It is helpful to consider how staff define and recognize students' positive self-esteem and how this behaviour can be fostered in all pupils, since the same strategies can be applied to any child. The following activities would be appropriate for staff training in self-esteem and resilience, working in small groups or in pairs with plenary feedback sessions. (See also Rhodes & Ajmal, 1995) Staff can use their knowledge of pupil behaviour that displays signs of high self-esteem to identify the characteristics they hope to see more of in the future:

> *How do we recognize when a child has positive self-esteem?*
> *How do we recognize when a child is resilient?*
> *What tells us this in their work?*
> *What tells us this in the way they relate to each other?*
> *What tells us this in the way they relate to staff?*
> *How is high self-esteem and resilience related to their achievement in class?*

Staff can be made more aware of the various ways they already encourage self-esteem and resilience:

> *In what ways do we actively promote resilience and self-esteem?*
> *What activities in class promote a helpful self-confidence?*
> *What activities outside the classroom?*
> *What do we do to encourage these to happen?*
> *How do we support vulnerable pupils in school?*

Once this knowledge and skill is recognized, it is easier to identify signs of progress that would be significant:

> *When we are even better at promoting students' confidence, how will we know?*
> *What will be different for vulnerable students in school?*
> *What will staff be doing differently?*
> *Will parents notice anything different?*
> *What will they notice?*

The answers to these questions offer potentially important clues about building self-esteem. Promoting resilience is an aspect of anti-bullying where schools and students have some success already. Rigby (1996) found that for the majority of children who have been victims of bullying, it is 'a fairly transient experience'. Further, when asked how they felt about being bullied, just under a third of pupils who reported they were bullied at least once a week said that they 'weren't really bothered'. Solution-focused questions can pursue exactly how staff can encourage this resilience.

### Training on self-esteem

In a recent training session, staff in a primary school worked in groups of four or five, each concentrating on a different aspect of children's social development. One group had chosen 'raising self-esteem' and within five minutes they had listed the following examples of their existing practice:

Reward systems and merits; Certificates in assembly; Providing work at the right level of difficulty; Praise; Buddy system; School council; Nurture group; Extra-curricular activities; Clubs; Welcoming new children into class; Looking after visitors; Stories; Staff showing by example; Assembly; Playtime games; Working in groups; Sharing resources; Displays of work; Photographs; Realistic targets; Self-assessment.

When staff participate in training that draws attention to what they already do, they are often surprised by the range of different activities. It is a means of sharing ideas and acts as a reminder of what they already know about that works.

## Summary

Instead of taking a detour around solving the problem, a low incidence of bullying can be achieved by schools planning to provide an environment that is friendly, safe and supportive.

Examples have been given of how group activities in training and individual conversations are able to recognize the things staff are already doing, and to plan specific areas for improvement using solution-focused techniques.

Solution-focused schools provide the most important and powerful insulation against bullying by ensuring that present good practice is appreciated. Staff can capitalise on the skills they have available to ensure progress towards their vision of how they want their school to be. This is achieved by continually asking themselves and others questions that build their confidence to do more of what works. In this way, all members of the school community not only contribute to the vision of the school, they can also be acknowledged for the role they play in helping to achieve it.

# CHAPTER 3
# CLASSROOM WORK

## Introduction

The previous chapter described how solution-focused professional development reinforces existing good practice and generates useful suggestions at a whole-school level. It inevitably included some ideas relevant to promoting an anti-bullying ethos in the classroom, such as teachers modelling good social skills and promoting pupils' self-esteem. Methods of teaching can be chosen that promote mutual cooperation and support and implicitly contribute to anti-bullying in all areas of the curriculum. Solution-focused discussions in the classroom can reduce bullying by diverting attention to what will be different when relations between students are better. This chapter includes examples of such conversations and also describes recent work in using classroom coaching to enhance both personal skills and learning.

## Classroom climate

Schools are acutely aware of the need to carefully assess outcomes whenever an initiative introduces additional curriculum work taking up time previously spent teaching something else. For this reason, promoting a friendly and supportive ethos should be incorporated whenever possible into the day-to-day management of teaching and learning in the classroom.

Existing programmes for health, personal and social education and citizenship often include lesson plans to teach children about bullying and many anti-bullying projects also recommend stories or drama featuring bullying. However, Pepler (Harachi et al., 1999) led a study in Canada that showed children already generally understood the concept of bullying appropriate to their age, without it needing to be taught.

Project evaluations have shown that talking about it will not necessarily reduce bullying and under some circumstances may even lead to an increase.

To avoid giving attention to and reinforcing unwanted behaviour, it is better that stories do not concentrate specifically on bullying in schools. Traditional children's tales abound with friends and foes, bullies and victims, but in an imaginative context. In my own project, promoting friendship through storytelling, we found that pupils had an understanding of bullying good enough to obviate any need to teach about it. We concentrated on team-building games, collaborative work in groups and pairs, circle-time discussions about friendship and mutual support – themes illustrated throughout by short stories. Teachers have routinely used stories, drama and film in this indirect way, avoiding any obvious moralising that might lead to resistance, whilst assisting students to envisage how they would like to be, both in and out of school.

In Norway, Galloway and Roland (2004), concerned about the efficiency and sustainability of traditional 'bullying-focused' interventions, based their anti-bullying programme on improving the quality of teaching and learning. They maintained that anti-bullying initiatives should assist teachers with their core work in the classroom rather than emphasize bullying. The SAVE anti-bullying project in Spain made *convivencia* central to their approach. They define the concept of *convivencia* as, 'a spirit of solidarity, fraternity, cooperation, harmony, a desire for mutual understanding, the desire to get on well with others, and the resolution of conflict through dialogue or other non-violent means.' By promoting *convivencia* and improving interpersonal relationships in classrooms, teachers also achieved significant reductions in bullying (Ortega, Del Ray & Mora-Merchan, 2004, p169).

The methods used to deliver the curriculum are arguably more powerful than the content in contributing to positive relationships between students. For example, any truly collaborative group work – not simply pupils doing individual work while sitting in groups – is an anti-bullying activity because it offers a method of learning that validates and encourages mutual support. Left to chance, pupils tend to confine their interactions to relatively few other children, mostly of the same gender. They can go through a year or more of school, socialising in the same small circle while hardly ever speaking to others in the class unless there is a deliberate effort to encourage students to work together and develop a supportive group identity. By engaging them in cooperative working, teaching and learning incorporates the development of improved social skills such as active listening and respecting others' opinions, regardless of the topic.

Ever more teachers are encouraging positive social interaction within students' normal working routines in the classroom because it is increasingly recognized as an effective strategy to enhance learning. Successful teaching and learning can reduce bullying without necessarily giving it any explicit attention.

### Secret Friends

This is a class-wide strategy that I first heard about from staff working in an excellent solution-focused primary school in Stockholm. Each member of the class draws out the name of someone who is to be their 'secret friend' for the coming week. During circle-time at the end of the week, the children try and guess who their secret friend was and what they had noticed that made them suspect so.

This is a lovely idea, teaching children implicitly the kind of favours friends do for each other and how these can be a matter of choice, not just accident. There are countless ways of extending this idea – maybe sometimes focusing several children on one child in the class for a week. This has the potential to provide support in a flexible and unobtrusive way, as part of the ongoing class development of social skills. It develops the same ethos as support groups described later in Chapter 5.

(Thanks to advisory teacher Martina Sundelin and Maria Mitra Ekstrom, headteacher at Lundskolan, Stockholm)

## Solution-focused anti-bullying discussions

Where the aim of a discussion is to reduce bullying, solution-focused conversations help by directing attention away from bullying and towards what is wanted instead, so that participants concentrate on reinforcing good social skills.

Questions from the teacher to the class about the preferred future invite children to describe how they would like relationships in their class or group to be:

*Imagine everyone in this class has a brilliant week …*
*How will students be behaving towards each other?*
*What will be different?*

*When this class is at its best, how do you treat each other?*
*How do you manage that?*
*How will this help your learning?*

*How will you know when this class is as friendly as you would like it*
*to be?*
*What will you notice happening more?*
*What is the first thing I will notice?*

*What will other teachers see that will tell them this is a happy and*
*supportive class to be in?*
*What will your parents/carers notice that will tell them you are happy*
*at school?*

When students describe the preferred future in terms of what will not be happening, their views should be fully acknowledged before moving on to ask what they want instead. If a pupil says, for example:

*No-one will be calling other people names.*

An effective response is:

*Yes, good, that's right! So what will be happening instead, when no-one*
*is calling other people names? How will everyone be talking to each*
*other?*
*How will this help you?*
*How will this help the class?*

Inquiring about the successful past recognizes what pupils are doing already and reminds them of their positive behaviour towards each other.

*How does your friendliness and support show itself in this class at*
*present?*
*What exactly do you do to help each other?*
*With a partner, think of ten different ways members of this class support*
*each other.*

## A class circle-time discussion

In one session, during a discussion about how they would like their class to be, I asked the students to watch out for anyone doing anything that helped the class to be more friendly, so we could talk about it the following week. The next week's discussion took a surprising turn.

One student, Peter, said that David had helped. David immediately sat up and listened. His nomination was unexpected for all of us because at the time David was receiving extra support from a classroom assistant because of his aggressive behaviour. Peter was asked to say what exactly he had noticed and he started, 'David hasn't been bullying me this week.' He continued by describing how David had been friendly when they had shared some equipment. As with all the students who made suggestions, Peter was complimented for noticing and remembering this example and David was praised for being so kind. The discussion moved on to someone else.

What this showed me was that anyone in the class, even those one might least expect, can gain attention for their better behaviour given an opportunity such as this. About three weeks later, when his education plan was being reviewed, a different teacher mentioned how David was making progress and gave an example of him acting more gently when helping Peter in the group. It seemed likely that Peter nominating him for very similar behaviour had encouraged David to maintain it.

Specific examples of how pupils help or have been helped by someone else when they were in need of support are useful:

*Think of a time recently when you were unhappy about something and someone in this class helped you...*
*What exactly did they do?*
*How did that help?*
*How do you help someone else who isn't happy?*
*What do you do?*
*How do you know it works?*

And they can remind themselves about the occasions when they managed to make amends:

*If someone realises they have been unfriendly, how can they try to put it right afterwards?*

Solution-focused conversation avoids 'zooming in' on unpleasant feelings such as anger or jealousy or being frightened or upset. On the contrary, it 'normalises' unpleasant feelings and affirms children's abilities to overcome them by assuming competence.

*Anyone can feel angry at times ...*

*When you have been angry, how did you manage to calm yourself down?*

*How did that help?*

*What happened as a result?*


*If someone has been unpleasant, how do you cope with it?*

*How do others help?*

From their own past experiences and those of others, students can inform themselves about possible alternatives for handling difficult situations in the future. Individual students or the class as a whole can be complimented directly on their actions mentioned in discussions, or by reference to other good behaviour the teacher has noticed in school. Any appreciation will tend to encourage students to use these strengths even more in the future.

*I am impressed by the way ...*

*This class is particularly good at ...*

*This lesson I have been pleased to see how you all ... most of you ...*

*I was proud of the way you ...*

The attention given to recognising the students' successful past and appreciating their strengths will reinforce this behaviour so that it tends to grow. The following questions help students to focus more narrowly on particular aspects the teacher may wish to target for further development:

*Think of one thing you will do this week to help make this class even more like you want it to be.*

*What will I notice about you?*

*Who else will notice?*

*What will they notice?*

Although conversations like these can be planned into the curriculum deliberately, they can just as well be used whenever it seems appropriate as part of a normal lesson. None of these questions are designed to lead to a prolonged discussion and certainly not one about bullying. I am reminded of watching a student teacher's lesson that began by his warning the class:

> *This lesson, I don't want you shouting out across the class while I'm talking. I don't want you to be throwing pencils around the room, or flicking rulers. I don't want you poking or kicking each other, or wandering round the room. What else should you not be doing in this lesson?*

Presumably the previous lesson had been something of a trial – this one certainly was! Experienced teachers know that drawing attention to what you do not want is asking for trouble. They know they can avoid doing this by focusing on what is wanted instead.

The aim of any discussion in the classroom regarding sensitive personal issues such as bullying is not to encourage children to ruminate on negative feelings such as anger, shame or guilt, which risks raising unnecessary fears or worse, inappropriate excitement. Solution-focused conversation is marked out by an optimistic lightness of touch, clearly describing what is wanted and giving pupils confidence in their own abilities, in this case to succeed in their relationships with others at school.

## Classroom coaching

Shilts & Berg have devised a simple and flexible style of solution-focused class coaching they call WOWW, or 'Working On What Works' (Shilts, 2008; See also Måhlberg & Sjöblom, 2008, 2009). Although previously people have experimented with solution-focused work in classrooms, this development has drawn added attention to the potential of coaching whole classes to improve their learning and behaviour.

The basic starting point is a member of staff observing someone else's lesson with an 'appreciative eye' (Annis Hammond, 1996, p. 6). At the beginning, the coach tells the pupils they will be watching and writing down anything they do, as a class or as individuals, that helps their learning. At the end of the lesson they will be told what has been noticed. The coach can usually find lots of examples, such as students working well together, using equipment carefully and listening respectfully to each other or the teacher. About ten minutes before the end, the coach gives positive feedback to the class about any constructive behaviour that has been noted. After the lesson, the coach may also compliment the teacher on a couple of things the teacher did that helped the pupils' learning, too.

In later coaching sessions, scaling can be used to help the class describe what they already manage to do well and the feedback can be extended to include suggestions from the class about what they would like to be doing more, or differently, to improve their learning in the future. The classroom coach can watch for any improvement in further sessions, or the students can be asked to watch out for it themselves in other lessons or during the coaching session itself.

Typically, teachers say classroom coaching makes them more aware of how well most of the students are learning, in ways that they may take for granted or not even notice in their day-to-day, busy role of teaching. Once the coaching feedback has drawn their attention to what is going well, students start to notice it more themselves and as a result become more positive in the classroom.

Based on our experience as teachers, the general assumption is that student behaviour needs to be actively controlled, or at least 'managed' in the classroom, otherwise it will naturally deteriorate. Yet during classroom coaching, when their learning behaviour was so clearly appreciated and pupils contributed to decisions about what they wanted to improve, they also began to take some of the responsibility for making the changes happen.

The outcomes of class coaching have included pupils becoming more pleasant and helpful and generally improving the way they relate to each other in class. For this reason solution-focused classroom coaching can be viewed as an anti-bullying activity, contributing significantly to positive relationships in the classroom and learning at the same time.

## Classroom coaching in a secondary school

This is an example of two sessions of coaching in a secondary school class of students aged 13-14. Although this class was the lowest set for ability, their teacher already managed their behaviour very well.

The teacher had been given information earlier in preparation for the session. After being introduced at the beginning, I told the class I would be watching for anything that was helpful to their learning, writing it down and telling them at the end of the lesson what I had noticed. The feedback to the class included:

- Everyone in the class followed instructions straight away, e.g. when told to use text books, everyone immediately picked up their books to find the right page.
- Students asked for help when they needed it, quietly and politely, avoiding distracting others.
- When the lesson was interrupted by a message for the teacher, there was no loss of concentration; they all returned to the task straight away afterwards.
- All students listened to each others' answers to the teacher.
- Several students contributed helpfully to the general smooth running of the class, getting pencils, taking a booklet, and gathering in books.

Towards the end of the second session, I did a solution-focused scaling exercise with the class, just before the feedback.

*On a scale of 1 to 10 where 10 is 'the best this class can be at learning', and 1 is 'learning nothing', where would they place the lesson they have just done?*

They agreed that lesson was about 7½.

*So what made it as high as 7½?*
- Doing games, different activities
- A good teacher
  - Makes you happy
  - Likes teaching
  - Helpful
  - Can have a laugh
- Listening when the teacher's talking
- Doing what the teacher asks

- Well prepared and organised

  *So if it were 8½ next time, what will be different for you to say that?*
  *What will you be doing differently to now?*
- Listening better
- Concentrating
- Working harder
- Putting up hands more
- Even more effort

  *So will it be possible to be 8½ next lesson? Would you like to try?*
  There was general agreement from the class – yes to both.

Feedback to the class from the second lesson included:
- When I arrived everyone was quietly listening to the teacher
- Everyone worked cooperatively with each other
- When the teacher said she didn't want something discussed during the lesson, the students turned back to their work straight away
- Students put up hands to answer questions as appropriate
- During some distracting behaviour, other students remained on task, concentrating on what they were doing

The teacher recognized a tangible difference in the class following coaching, for example she felt she could ask for volunteers to collect in books, whereas before she would have specified particular students to avoid several jumping up or shouting out. She also thought she had seen a noticeable improvement in their attitude to learning. Even though her classroom management was already very good, the teacher felt she had improved the way she was responding to students. She had been praising the students more consistently throughout their lessons and praising more non-work related behaviour such as helping in class and had already noticed the impact this was having on all her classes, not just this one. Students were responding better and becoming even more willing to work and cooperate during lessons.

(Thanks to the teacher, Rachel Cope, for allowing inclusion of this example.)

The same strategy can be used when a teacher identifies that a class has difficulties with their behaviour. The coach can watch out for any behaviour in particular the teacher wants to encourage. However, as this example suggests, any class can benefit from solution-focused coaching.

## Breaktimes

Several larger anti-bullying programmes have identified that lunchtime supervisor training and school grounds improvements may be helpful in decreasing bullying (Smith & Sharp, 1994; Ttofi, Farrington & Baldry, 2008). Primary school playground environments have improved markedly in recent years. There is much more likely to be seating available, play equipment provided, imaginative planting schemes and separate areas for games such as football. Secondary schools usually want to provide an environment more suggestive of a stimulating workplace. There are many possibilities for improving a school's physical environment to encourage constructive play and provide a valuable resource for learning. This is a good example of where pupils can be actively involved in suggesting and planning improvements on an ongoing basis.

Unstructured periods in school include breaks and lunchtimes, the times immediately before and after school and also moving around the school between lessons. What happens then is particularly pertinent to helping students feel safe because pupils are obviously under looser supervision. Given the right circumstances, these periods can also allow friendships to flourish and peer support to be most active.

The following example shows how a discussion can help when there has been a problem in school. The same conversations can be used preventatively to help pupils take responsibility and make breaktimes more enjoyable.

### Dealing with concerns following a break

A primary teacher told me how at the end of one particularly difficult playtime several of her class had been in trouble for fighting. As she led the class back to their room, she said she was 'fuming' and thinking about how she would give them a good telling off when they got inside. She had recently been on a training course and thought, 'What if I take a solution-focused approach, what would I be saying?'

'Thankfully,' she said laughing, 'it was a long corridor and I decided to have a go at trying to deal with it differently.' She asked the pupils to get into a circle and told them she was not happy with how some of the class had behaved and she supposed that they were not happy with what had occurred either. She asked them to think about what happens when breaktimes are better:

*On a scale of 1 to 10, where 1 is 'breaktimes are terrible, everybody is glad when they are over', and 10 is 'breaktimes are really great' ... Imagine breaktimes are 10 ...*

*What tells you it is so good?*
*What are you doing when breaks go well?*
*What do you notice others in this class doing?*

*Where would you normally place breaktime in this school on this scale?*
*What makes it so high?*
*What do you like best about breaks at this school?*

*What do you think I notice about you when you come back to class after you have had a good break?*

After talking about this for a short while she complimented the students on being able to recognize what they needed to do to enjoy the breaks. She said she was confident the next break would be much better.

The teacher reflected that this had been a much better way of dealing with the situation. She felt she had addressed the concerns without getting angry and instead there had been a very good, constructive discussion and they all felt better and able to get down to work afterwards without any continuing resentment affecting the lesson. By addressing the problem in this way, her relationship with the class had been strengthened rather than strained.

Pupils can be encouraged to take a pro-active role in creating a friendly and supportive school community during breaktimes. A peer-support scheme at Acland Burghley (Secondary) School in London was originally set up to help students to combat bullying. Their volunteer 'counsellors' underwent a training programme based on solution-focused practice and their excellent scheme was recognized in a video accompanying government anti-bullying guidance (DfEE, 2001). Further details can be found in Hillel & Smith (2001).

Many primary schools have introduced 'buddy' schemes to support pupils at breaktimes. Volunteers, usually sought from older year groups, will help any child who needs befriending. Buddies often wear something distinctive in the playground, such as caps or sweatshirts, to make themselves obvious to younger pupils. Peer support can help pupils who feel vulnerable yet do not want to tell an adult that they are struggling, which is often the case with bullying as well as other worries they may have. This way is simply more accessible and acceptable to pupils.

When pupils have volunteered to act as 'buddies' on the playground, they are often given some training to help prepare them for their role. Although the administrative detail will differ according to the school – and children may be asked to contribute their ideas to that too – all potential buddies would benefit from having their existing helping skills brought to the fore by talking about examples of how they have helped someone else in the past:

*How have you been a friend to someone you didn't know very well?*
*What exactly did you do?*
*How did this help?*
*How do you know it helped?*

*What is it about yourself that tells you that you can be a good*
  *playtime buddy?*
*Tell us one thing about the person sitting next to you that tells you they*
  *will make a good playground buddy.*

*What will you be doing differently when you are a playground buddy?*
*What difference will this make to breaktimes in this school?*

Their training includes recognising when they may need to involve staff:

*If anyone is worried about someone at breaktime, what is the best action*
  *to take?*
*And what if you are still worried?*

When schools puts systems of peer support in place they demonstrate and promote the caring ethos in school, although there needs to be close supervision so adult help is still there for pupils who need it and so peer helpers are fully supported.

## Summary

There are many ways existing good practice in the classroom can improve mutual support and reduce bullying behaviour without making any direct reference to it. Involving groups of pupils in positive social interaction is a direct and powerful way of promoting an anti-bullying environment both within class and beyond.

Just as a whole-school approach does not need to focus on bullying in order to reduce it, neither does an anti-bullying curriculum. Discussions about bullying will not necessarily lead to a lessening of bullying and may inadvertently increase it, unless they draw attention to what is wanted instead.

Most recently, classroom coaching has proved a very promising new strategy for improving pupils' classroom relationships and encouraging a better learning atmosphere. In a solution-focused school, staff and pupils are empowered to recognize and use the skills they already possess to enable the classroom climate to become more like they would both prefer it to be.

Just as solution-focused anti-bullying is efficient of staff time and effort at a whole-school level, it is also efficient with teachers' and pupils' time in the classroom because it capitalises on their existing capacity to foster a safe, friendly and supportive classroom environment that promotes learning. For the same reasons it is also more sustainable.

Despite all this, there may still be occasions when individual pupils need further support and we turn to ways of responding to individual incidents of bullying in the next three chapters.

# CHAPTER 4
# RESPONDING TO INCIDENTS

## Introduction

Previous chapters have demonstrated how solution-focused discussion can promote an anti-bullying culture at a whole-school and classroom level. Schools will tend to experience fewer serious incidents of bullying when they focus attention on a safe, supportive and friendly community. This chapter examines individual interventions where actual complaints about bullying are reported. Many 'low-level' strategies are already used to good effect in schools and the fact that they are normally effective means they attract little attention in the literature about bullying. At the same time, schools have recognized that some instances of bullying – or even of alleged bullying – can be tricky to bring to a successful conclusion (and maintaining good relationships with parents can become difficult when dealing with incidents of persistent bullying) so they look to more specialist strategies to help in such cases.

## Existing successful practice

Even when teachers do not intervene directly, they contribute to the self-esteem of all their pupils in a variety of ways, as already shown. When a child reacts in a confident manner to minor teasing, this is normally enough to stop it and there is no need to 'tell' anyone. Preventative work reduces, as intended, the number of minor incidents brought to staff, because pupils manage to sort them out for them-

FOUR: Responding to Incidents · 63

selves, and get on with their lives in school. This resilience is entirely commendable and should be encouraged.

However, established patterns of behaviour can be difficult to escape, especially when reinforced by the expectations and the needs of others present. Given the right circumstances, everyone is capable of acting as a bully, victim or bystander to some extent. What sets apart an effective school is not whether bullying occurs, but how it is dealt with when it does. All the advice and information available cannot replace the wealth of experience in dealing with children that staff are able to draw on.

In solution-focused terms, the successful past and present is achieved when people have responded well to incidents, any bullying has ceased and escalation has been avoided. We need to notice the ways in which staff respond effectively because this is where useful skills are most evident – bringing about successful outcomes before a pattern of bullying becomes ingrained. These strategies need to be valued and used in future practice; to enable what de Shazer called 'doing more of what works'.

When we look into cases of prolonged bullying, we understandably search for what went wrong. Although the strategies used were clearly ineffective in these cases at the time, we can only speculate about what might have worked instead. Since we know that most bullying in school is transient, getting beyond speculation and recognising existing, successful practice provides a real 'evidence-base' on which to build.

If a student approaches a member of staff for support following an isolated or relatively minor incident, a low level response is best, at least in the first instance. As children learn how to take part in social interactions, they will inevitably make mistakes and sometimes behave in a way that is not in accord with the values the school wants to promote. This behaviour may prove distressing to others or even to themselves and can happen for a host of different and complicated reasons, or perhaps due to chance and circumstance. So knowing the reasons why a problem has arisen, although interesting, does not necessarily help when trying to put it right. Although pupils need to know their concerns will be taken seriously, no student will thank someone for over-reacting to their request for help. Any response needs to be proportionate and use the lightest touch that works. Experienced

teachers and support staff are well practised at showing a caring attitude and responding sensitively to day-to-day complaints.

## Low-level responses

Schools may wish to include in the anti-bullying policy strategies for
dealing with minor complaints as well as a procedure to deal with
more serious bullying. The best way to do this is to gather together
ideas arising from discussions with staff who deal with minor incidents
on a regular basis:

> *When a pupil first makes a complaint that they have been bullied, or*
> *bothered by another pupil's behaviour towards them in any way, what*
> *are the best outcomes we hope to achieve?*
> *What difference will this make to us?*
> *What difference will this make to pupils?*
> *What difference will this make to parents?*
>
> *The last time you dealt well with a complaint of bullying, what exactly*
> *did you do?*
> *What were the signs that told you that you had handled it well?*
> *What helped you deal with the incident so well?*
> *What was it about your attitude that helped?*

One advantage of holding this discussion is that existing skills are
shared so that any member of staff can incorporate them into their
own practice. It appreciates the ongoing good work in the school and
thereby reinforces it. Any further action can build on this, with a clear
direction toward the best outcomes.

Typically, effective responses to day-to-day complaints of bullying
usually include:

- Asking another pupil, or pupils, to accompany someone who is
  feeling vulnerable for a while. Some schools have organised systems
  of peer support along these lines.
- Speaking to a student who has been the subject of a complaint
  to raise their awareness that someone may have been troubled by
  something they did, even though it may have been unintended.

The last response is an example of 'positive connotation'. Many teachers use this in dealing with low-level behaviour difficulties. When a member of staff deliberately construes a pupil's action as neutral, or even positive, it encourages cooperation and avoids pupils becoming defensive and resistant to changing their behaviour (Molnar & Lindquist, 1989). It is particularly useful for dealing with complaints of bullying, where resentment can easily be aroused against a pupil who 'tells' on someone, because it enables the teacher to intervene without pre-judging the situation. A teacher can imply the behaviour could have been over-enthusiastic play or meant as a joke. These are credible connotations because when pupils are confronted with accusations of bullying, they often maintain they were 'only having a laugh' or 'just playing':

> *I can see you are enjoying your playtime ... and I know you wouldn't*
> *want to hurt anyone, would you?*
> *So maybe you could settle it down a bit?*
> *Thanks – that's helpful!*

> *I know you have a lively sense of humour but I want to let you know*
> *that another student has found it hurtful.*
> *I am sure this is not your intention, is it?*
> *So maybe you will want to be a bit more careful?*
> *Thank you – I think you can manage to sort this out yourself!*

Dealing with the situation in this way avoids accusation and counter-arguments and implies a number of useful assumptions. It lets the pupil know that a potential difficulty has been noted. They may have considered their behaviour as reasonable under other circumstances, but now it has been pointed out that someone else has a problem with it, the assumption is that the student will agree to change their behaviour. Dealing with the situation in this way makes it reasonable for the teacher to check later that any issue has been resolved and gives an opportunity to praise both parties for sorting it out themselves. This reinforces the resolution of any difficulty.

Of course, there can be no guarantee, but as we have seen, when the assumptions behind any enquiry are both appreciative and credible at the time, it is more likely to be useful for bringing about change.

## Happiness Detectives

This is a strategy that has been used for supporting children in primary school who may be vulnerable.

A child can choose up to five classmates who all form a group together. The group is asked if they would like to be 'happiness detectives' taking part in a 'mission' that involves watching out for anyone doing anything that makes the school a happier place. They are encouraged to make suggestions about some of the ways this might happen and all their ideas are complimented and written up on a board or flip-chart. The following week the unhappy child is seen first, followed by the whole group to review their mission. Usually, the children talk proudly about what they have done and what they have noticed other members of the group doing to help make others happy. These meetings usually carry on for about five weeks before the children are confident they can continue the mission independently. There is a celebration with certificates for everyone in the group. Teachers have found that all children who become 'happiness detectives' benefit through increased social skills, higher levels of confidence and classroom co-operation. This is an approach that can be used even when there is no single individual who is in need of support.

(Thanks to Declan Coogan, Senior Social Worker and Family Therapist, Dublin, for this adaptation of support groups.)

If any bullying appears to be more serious, if difficulties continue or if a member of staff is unsure whether a more active response is called for, it is useful to find out from the person feeling bullied:

*Is this something they can manage to sort out on their own, or do they need help to resolve it?*
*Have they had this difficulty before?*

The answers to these questions will clarify if further action is needed. Bullying incidents, like other unwanted behaviour, lie on a continuum, from mild teasing that may have been unintentionally hurtful, to daily physical or emotional tormenting. The question of extended bullying is important because once a pupil feels bullied, any ensuing level of harassment may appear mild even to the point of absurdity, such as 'someone keeps looking at me', yet can be just as intimidating for the student.

Although low-level intervention is often all that is required, once a pattern of bullying is established – if the situation is ongoing or deteriorating, or a parent has informed the school that their child is being bullied – staff will want to lead and monitor any intervention themselves.

## Parental involvement

Any approach benefits from the support of parents, not only those of the victim, but also the parents of children who may have been bullying others or indeed may have been unjustly accused. Often, particularly in primary school, an initial complaint about a child struggling with bullying will come from a parent. Part of responding effectively to serious bullying incidents is engaging successfully with parents. When a parent is worried that their child is being bullied in school it can be extremely distressing. A parent may be concerned about unusual behaviour at home that may not be apparent in school – irritability to the point of violent outbursts, bed wetting, sleep difficulties or minor aches and pains in the morning. These signs of stress may have been apparent for some time before a child tells a parent that they feel frightened by other pupils in school. Parents often fear that complaining may make matters worse and their child may well ask them not to tell the school anything. Parents report strong feelings of powerlessness and frustration in this situation. By the time they decide they must speak to someone at the school they are often very anxious and may even exaggerate their complaint in an attempt to provoke a satisfactory response. Furthermore, parents often feel defensive regarding anything they imagine might have made their child a target of bullying, such as clothes or shoes.

Although at first parents may demand severe punishment, such as exclusion, this is because they assume punishment is the only course of action that will stop the bullying, even if sanctions have not worked in the past. Parents are usually willing to go along with alternative suggestions so long as they feel assured that their concern is being taken seriously and will be acted on. It is effectiveness they want, rather than revenge or retribution.

It is perhaps not surprising, given the adverse publicity and possible legal action that could ensue, that schools can also become defensive when dealing with a complaint of bullying. Instead of giving attention to the parent's concerns, they sometimes respond by minimising the problem, for example by dismissing the idea that there is any serious bullying at the school. This kind of response can make a parent feel anxious and ignored, and more likely to go somewhere else for help and support, even though the best chance of bringing about a successful resolution lies within the school. Even when the initial response to a parent has been reassuring, if the action taken does not stop the bullying, or if as often happens it later resumes, the blame tends to shift from the bully to the victim and/or the victim's parents. Parents of bullied children can easily become viewed as 'over-protective', or their child can be seen as 'provocative'. Unfortunately this can contribute to the development of a vicious circle.

The perceptions of the parent will contribute to the ease or difficulty of finding a solution. Clearly, if a child is unhappy at school there is a need for action, whatever the cause. Instead of becoming defensive, school staff can respond positively, without 'admitting' to anything other than being a caring community. An effective school can use a parental complaint as an opportunity to demonstrate the supportive ethos of the school.

Parents find it helpful to be introduced to the person who will take day-to-day responsibility for any intervention and who can be the main point of contact. Teaching assistants are often very effective at dealing with bullying, since they often have more time and flexibility than teaching staff. Parents can provide valuable information on the happiness of their child, so staff dealing with the situation need to let parents know they value their opinion. Once the bullying is resolved, parents will value being thanked for their patience and cooperation during a difficult time.

The skill of a solution-focused approach lies in enabling pupils and their parents to understand and realise their potential for bringing about change for the better. Presupposing and reinforcing a partnership approach with both the parents and the pupils is creative, rewarding for all concerned and ultimately more successful.

## Responding to more 'serious' bullying

Anti bullying is part of the 'inclusion' agenda in schools. Interventions to eliminate bullying situations in school should share the same values underpinning inclusion. Exclusion from school is not an anti-bullying strategy but a last resort in extreme cases where attempts made to resolve the situation have failed, placing other students' safety seriously at risk. In such cases the headteacher may need to consider, in consultation with parents and other interested child welfare agencies, whether a student's behaviour constitutes criminal assault and needs to be reported to the police.

Some students are so vulnerable they need specialist support beyond the remit of school staff. Every year in the UK several students commit suicide where bullying at school appears to be a contributory factor. If any pupil appears to be struggling in school despite the existing support system – to the extent that they withdraw themselves completely from social situations or the staff fear they may harm themselves – then an urgent referral to specialist health or welfare services is required.

Thankfully, most 'bullies' and 'victims' are simply ordinary pupils who have made an error of judgement or been caught at a vulnerable time. Most bullying in schools can be alleviated once it is addressed. Providing a context and expectation of change using parents' and pupils' positive contributions is helpful in making it happen, to everyone's benefit.

When there is clear evidence that one student has deliberately hurt another in any way, then *not* to make it clear that such behaviour is unacceptable would contradict a sense of justice that most people, including teachers, children and parents, would consider right and proper. Bullying can be dealt with in the usual manner according to the school behaviour policy. Any restorative action or sanctions should be proportionate and use the lightest touch that works. The only way of gauging success is to check there has been no recurrence.

Traditionally, the recommended approach to resolving a complaint about bullying involves investigating what has been going on, forming a judgement based on the evidence and putting in place a strategy to stop it, often involving some kind of sanction. Examples of these approaches could include keeping the 'bully' inside for a given number of days at breaktimes, or reporting the behaviour to parents. Unfortunately, as many teachers have discovered, this is often not as straightforward as it sounds. Bullying is not so amenable to teacher influence because in some sense it is the pupils' business. As bullying usually happens away from staff supervision, the result of an investigation can often come down to believing one child's word against another and adults are quite rightly reluctant to punish pupils without clear evidence. One of the reasons for children not reporting bullying to adults is their fear that punishment may exacerbate instead of resolve the situation.

Pupils need to be able to ask for help with confidence that any action taken will keep them safe. Yet teachers, parents and pupils are often worried that responding to a complaint about bullying, even when punishment is not used, may lead to resentment and more bullying in the future, perhaps in a subtler form that makes it even more difficult to control. To avoid this risk, teachers sometimes try to keep a closer eye on what is happening so they can intervene directly from their own observation. Sometimes students worried by bullying are allowed access to an area under closer supervision at breaktimes or there are attempts to separate pupils, even moving students to another class. In extreme cases parents have changed their child's school. Although these strategies sometimes work insofar as they break a pattern of behaviour, they do not necessarily provide a longer-term solution and can even reinforce an unacceptable situation.

Since students are generally reluctant to complain about being bullied, it follows that when they do ask for help, it may be a sign that intervention is urgent. Providing traditional counselling or social skills training, usually for a victim, can take weeks before progress is made. It also carries the unfortunate implication that the victim is somehow at fault or needs to change. When young people are referred to an outside agency, including phone help-lines or internet sites, there needs to be clear accountability. Some schools may have ready access to another agency or anti-bullying project that will provide immediate support from outside, but in practice most schools do not have this option. For these reasons schools have sought strategies they can implement themselves that deal adequately and speedily with more serious bullying and at the same time avoid risks.

The best-known strategies devised specifically to address bullying include the 'Method of Shared Concern' developed in Norway by Pikas (1989) and the 'No Blame Approach' from Maines and Robinson (1992). These assume that bullying has taken place and it is known who is responsible. Pikas was the first to recognize the importance of the wider 'bully-group' in stopping bullying and he also recommended encouraging individual members of the group to make suggestions to resolve the issue rather than investigating the details of what had been happening and using punishment. However, this is a rather elaborate approach that needs specialist training and a considerable amount of time. The 'No Blame Approach' was simpler and therefore more accessible and quicker to put into action, and so has become better known, at least in England. Victims are encouraged to describe their feelings about being bullied and write or draw a picture expressing them. These feelings are recounted to the group to raise empathy and to encourage group members to suggest ways that they can help. The pupils are then seen individually to monitor progress. Following widespread criticism, the authors changed the name of the 'No Blame Approach' several times, most recently to the 'Support Group Method'.

A solution-focused intervention 'stays on the surface' (de Shazer, 1994) and so avoids negative assumptions about anyone involved or reliance on hidden motivations. Consideration needs to be given to the potential adverse effects of encouraging someone who is already vulnerable to concentrate attention on describing their negative feelings (Craig, 2009). Also, the victim recounting to a group of pupils their heartfelt unhappiness disregards the possibility that details could be used in any future tormenting, not necessarily by someone involved in the original group. Since there are no need to take such risks, the possible consequences can easily be avoided. Solution-focused practice deliberately deflects attention away from negative feelings, towards positive actions and how existing skills and strengths can be used to bring them about. Any existing problem is left behind – the objective is not so much to solve a problem but to move beyond it.

It has generally been accepted that interventions involving pupils in a positive way can be very useful. Earlier in this chapter it was mentioned that staff in schools frequently use peer support success-fully to intervene at an early stage to prevent bullying. The use of peer support targeted on particular children and monitored more closely by staff is a practical example of extending existing good practice.

## 'Gary'

Gary's mother telephoned the local authority to ask what could be done about her child being bullied at school. She sounded obviously distressed as she spoke. Although reluctant, the headteacher agreed to outside agency involvement. I rang the mother the same day and arranged to meet both her and Gary the following afternoon and to speak to the headteacher afterwards.

Gary was 11 years old. His mum explained that he had started school with speech difficulties and although he had made progress he was still behind for his age in reading. He was also physically small for his age and had unexplained rashes on his hands. He was wetting the bed at night. Mum was anxious that she could not afford to buy Gary expensive fashionable clothes, but she always made sure that he was clean and tidy for school. Both mum and Gary became distressed. Gary was particularly distraught when I was told about the bedwetting. Apparently mum had tried to reason with the mother of one of the 'bullies' and had mentioned it. As a result the boys at school had found out and taunted him about it in the playground. The bullying had become worse and had started to happen outside school time in the street. That is when she phoned the police who in turn advised her to contact the local authority.

I outlined the support group approach and said that this could be appropriate – it would avoid provoking the resentment that might arise if anyone were punished. Gary was quite adamant that he did not want to return to school.

When I visited the school I talked to the headteacher and the teacher for special needs. They said that the victim's family had caused problems for the school. The younger sister was very disruptive in class and the father was aggressive, having to be escorted off the premises on one occasion. They were aware that Gary had been the subject of some taunting but were also aware that he was 'no angel' himself. They did try to deal with incidents as they happened.

I suggested a peer support group would be an appropriate way forward since no-one would be punished, possibly unfairly. The children involved would enjoy doing it and after all, it was the most effective approach that we know.

The children were called out of class and seen by myself with the special needs teacher. The group was aware that Gary was not happy in school but we did not pursue any reasons why this might be. A couple of the group said that they too had been unhappy in school in the past when they had been called names. When I asked if they had any suggestions for how to make him happier they were quite ready to come up with their own ideas. One suggested he would sit with Gary in the dining hall and another said he would watch for Gary at playtime to make sure he was not alone. A girl said she would talk to him. After each suggestion, I reassured them and praised them individually in various ways, e.g. 'That's a good idea! How did you manage to think of that?' or 'Have you done kind things like that for other people before?' Once I had suggestions from all of them, I thanked them, wished them luck and arranged to see them in a week's time to see how they were getting on.

It was difficult to persuade Gary to return to school. In the end, it was arranged that his mother would take him to school and only leave him when the whistle had gone in the playground. She would pick him up at lunchtime too. I said I would visit him in school in two days' time and I checked with his mother the day following the meeting that Gary had indeed returned to school. On the phone she sounded very anxious about what he might be suffering at school and warned me that if Gary was bullied that morning, she did not feel able to insist on him going back in the afternoon.

Two days later, I saw him briefly in school. When he came into the room to see me he smiled and said tearfully, 'I never knew I had so many friends.' When I went back a week later, he said things were 'even better' because 'they weren't so fussy any more – it was just normal.'

I saw the group without Gary and invited them to tell me if they had managed to help and if so, how. They told me, for example, how they had deliberately included him in games in the playground. I complimented each one for what they had done, e.g. the sensitive and careful way they had shown support. When I asked if they thought he was happier and how they did they know, they said he was smiling, talking more and laughing. They were congratulated on their wonderful plan and asked if they would keep going for another week. They were all very keen to continue.

I phoned his mother to ask how she felt he was getting along and she said that Gary was 'a different lad', enjoying school again. Gary had even insisted that she allow him to stay at school for lunch.

The following week everything was settled and fine. I took a photograph of the group and Gary together – as I said, I liked to have photographs of the best groups. I also arranged for the teacher to make sure they all received an appropriate school reward for their achievement. About a year later I was asked to help with another case in the same school. The teacher sat in again and has since regularly used the approach, with complete success.

(Adapted from Young, 2001)

Responding to bullying in a solution-focused way means that attention is focused on the details of what will be happening once it is resolved, i.e. the preferred future. This can be planned for by staff and students using what they already know about making pupils happier in school. The Support Group Approach (Young, 1998) is a solution-focused version of peer group intervention. Another intervention is to use solution-focused interviewing. Both of these have been shown to work. Evidence and experience suggests that, broadly speaking, support groups are particularly suited to younger, and mainly primary school pupils and solution-focused interviewing is particularly suitable for older, secondary school students. There is a detailed description of each of these approaches in Chapters 5 and 6 respectively.

## Summary

Low-level interventions are entirely appropriate for what we might call 'minor' bullying, and school staff are well used to intervening successfully at this stage. Action will need to be stepped up if the student continues to have difficulties or if the parents have informed the school their child is being bullied.

Engaging in a collaborative way with parents is an essential part of dealing effectively with more serious bullying. Parents also need time and consideration when they are placed in this position and solution-focused schools can use this as an opportunity to show how caring and supportive they are.

Special strategies to deal with bullying have developed because schools have in some cases found traditional behaviour management approaches to be ineffective. Any anti-bullying response must be seen as fair to both pupils and parents because this contributes to the sustainability of the most important outcome – the young person once again being happy in school. The next two chapters describe solution-focused interventions that provide effective support where bullying has become a problem for individual pupils.

# CHAPTER 5
# PEER SUPPORT GROUPS

## Introduction

This chapter begins with a quick summary of a method to lead solution-focused support groups for children feeling bullied that has been tried and tested extensively in primary schools (Young, 1998; 2001; 2008). For the sake of clarity, a straightforward situation is being used here as an example where a complaint about bullying has been made by a parent and the school wants to provide the child with support. Following a quick summary, there is a typical dialogue with accompanying notes of explanation. There is also information about the outcomes of using this approach and reflections on the experience in terms of partnerships with both pupils and parents.

## Quick summary

Throughout this intervention no assumptions are made about what has been happening, so using the words 'bully' or 'bullying' or 'victim' is unhelpful and avoided in the following description. Whoever is leading the intervention needs to interview the child who is finding life difficult in school in order to identify pupils who should be in the support group. The lead person could be either a teacher or a support assistant. Usually, a first interview will be held with the child in school. If the parent is present, it is helpful to ask if it is okay for their child to answer some questions, which signals it is the child's turn in the conversation. Parents can sometimes inadvertently act as their child's spokesperson, or indeed the child may feel they need to justify their parent's worries. Both parent and child need to feel confident that their concerns are being taken seriously and there is no need to question the validity of anyone's perspective. This is not an interview to investigate incidents or possible causes, or to identify who is to blame for the situation arising.

The lead person adopts the view, regardless of any rights and wrongs, that the child has become unhappy and that this in itself is a genuine concern requiring action.

### Interviewing the child to be supported
The aim of the interview is simply to find out who are the most appropriate pupils to be in the support group. The group will consist of pupils the child finds difficult, others who may have been around, and any friends. It can be accepted that the child needs support without any need for them to give any explanation or ask about their feelings – something that could be counter-productive.

### Meeting with the support group
The support group is selected from the names given by the child targeted for support. A support group typically consists of all the pupils whom the child finds difficult, two or three other children who seem to be around at the time and any friends or potential friends; in all, about five to eight children. Having a minimum of five pupils provides a range of different ideas and helps spread the responsibility. It also means there is likely to be someone from the support group nearby most of the time. More than eight pupils can make the process during the meeting a little slow and diminish the significance of any single pupil's contribution. If possible, it works well to mix gender and/or ethnicity. The aim of meeting with the support group is to let them know their help is needed and gain their commitment to the task of supporting someone else to be happy in school. Most of this meeting is spent encouraging and complimenting their suggestions.

### Review with the child being supported
About a week later, the child who is being supported is seen again for a review. This interview will concentrate on discovering what is better and congratulating the child on whatever they have managed to do differently that has helped. In this way the situation is monitored and any positive change is reinforced.

### Review with the support group
The interview with the group provides the opportunity to show appreciation for what they have been doing, both individually and as a

group. It also supplies another perspective from which to monitor the situation and judge whether it is necessary for the group to continue giving their support.

L = Lead person

S = Sam, the child in need of support

A-F = Members of the support group: Amed, Ben, Carl, Danny, Ethan, Freddie

## Interviewing the child to be supported

It is worth spending a couple of minutes at the start of the conversation on any subject other than the difficulties to avoid giving the impression that the child is viewed only as a problem.

Pupils may be anxious, expecting they will be asked to talk about what is a difficult and distressing subject for them. It helps to begin with questions that they will have no difficulty answering. The lead person can to be listening right from the outset for examples that might emerge of occasions when the child is happier in school.

LEAD: Hi, Sam, sorry to disturb you during lesson time ... what
       were you doing?
SAM: Maths.
  L: Oh yes ... What are you doing in maths at the moment?
  S: Circles and things.
  L: I used to enjoy that ... do you?
  S: It's okay.
  L: What do you enjoy most in school?
  S: I like reading and writing stories.
  L: Oh ... what book are you reading at the moment?

Introducing the main part of the session, it is respectful to ask if the child wants help and to gain their 'consent' for the interview and any intervention on their behalf. This helps build their confidence in someone else's involvement and lessens any sense of disempowerment they might feel in receiving help. It is well known that pupils feeling unhappy for any reason often find it difficult to tell someone. It is easier for them to admit that someone else is worried.

L: Right, I've been talking with your mum. She is worried that you are not so happy in school at present. Did you know she's worried?

S: *[Nods head]*

L: I think I will be able to help. Would you like my help with this?

S: Mmm.

L: I need to ask you a few questions if that's okay? I've noticed already you are good at answering questions!

S: Mmm.

The membership of a support group is based on the names given by the child. Note they are not asked, *Who is bullying you?* Occasionally, depending on their past experience, it may be necessary to reassure children that you are not asking them to 'tell tales'. Children are sensitive about getting anyone else into trouble, arguably with good reason.

L: I need to know who may be able to help. Who are you finding difficult in school at the moment?

S: Err ... I'm not sure I want to ...

L: Don't worry, I don't need to know any details, I just want to know who can help. Okay?

S: Okay. It's Amed...

L: Right ... Amed *[writing the name down]*

S: And Ben too sometimes...

L: ... and Ben *[writing it down]* Anyone else?

S: No, it's just them.

L: Okay, that's fine... Who else is around when things are difficult for you?

S: Carl is sometimes there. And Ethan, too.

L: Okay, Carl and Ethan ... anyone else?

S: Err ... Freddie sometimes ... No-one else.

L: Okay, that's good.

In primary school, usually between one and three other pupils are mentioned as being difficult for the child. As a general rule, the younger the child the fewer the number of children they find difficult. If more than four are nominated, they can be asked for 'the main ones'.

Whenever noting anything on paper, it is reassuring to a child if they can see what is being written.

There are usually other children around when a child is having difficulties. Commonly, two or three names are mentioned. Again, there is no need for elaboration – it can be accepted that other children are nearby without making any assumptions about whether they are involved.

L: And who is your friend in school?
S: Err … Amed is my friend.
L: Right, Amed. Anyone else?
S: *[Shakes head]*
L: Who else would you like to be your friend at school?
S: Ethan.

It is not unusual for a child to name someone they have already mentioned they are finding difficult, as a friend. I presume from this that bullying can often be a result of friendship gone awry. When asking about friends, the child can usually supply a couple of names. However, if the child has been struggling for some time, it is possible they may not be able to identify anyone as a friend. In which case, they can be asked whom they would *like* to have as a friend.

L: Okay, that's great … I've got all these names down now. Right, I am going to ask these children if they can help make things happier for you in school. I will want to see you again to find out how you are getting on, say next week. Is that okay?
S: Yes.
L: I am impressed by how brave you are, to come and talk with me about this so clearly. I am sure that things will begin to improve quite quickly. I will send for you again next Wednesday morning so you can tell me how you are getting on. Is that okay?
S: Okay.
L: Meanwhile, I want you to notice what's better so you can tell me all about it next week. Can you remember to do that?
S: Yeah …

L: Is there anything else you want to tell me?

S: No, I don't think so …

L: Good! I hope you haven't missed too much maths. Good luck! See you next week, bye!

S: Bye! *[The pupil goes back to class]*

After briefly telling the child what is going to happen, a review is arranged, usually for about a week later. If a pupil or parent is very anxious, an opportunity can be found to have a quick check even earlier. The conversation can end with compliments and a reassurance that things will improve. This generates hope and an expectation that things will be changing for the better straight away. Hopefulness and expectation are significant factors in bringing about change and can have a powerful influence on what will happen. Asking the pupil to notice and remember improvements so they can talk about them next time helps focus their attention on whatever is getting better.

As the interview comes to a close, a good question to ask is whether the pupil wants to say anything else. It is common for people to think that children will want to talk about the difficulties they have had. In fact, they often seem relieved at not having to go over it all again, or to 'tell tales' about other pupils. Regardless, this question gives them the opportunity to say whatever they like before they leave.

## Meeting with the support group

This meeting is best kept light and optimistic, rather than serious. The children are welcomed to the meeting, starting off with some non-problem talk, as before. Sometimes they may look a little nervous about what is going to happen and if so, they may need a bit of reassurance. The pupils might know if a parent has been into school and they are usually aware the child to be supported has just been seen, so they may be anticipating trouble; after all, children are not normally called out of class unless it is something 'serious'.

L: *[Smiling and welcoming]* Well, let's have a look at you all … you look very smart in your school sweatshirts! Is everyone here? Let me see … Amed, Ben, Carl, Danny, Ethan and Freddie. Yes … that's great! Have you enough room to sit

here? ... Can I see all your faces? ... Thank you, I'm pleased
to see you're all here.

A: Are we in trouble, Miss?

L: No, I just want your help, is that okay? *[group members nod]*
Thanks for coming, all of you! You may have noticed that
Sam is not too happy in school at the moment. I need your
help to make him feel happier. I have chosen you because I
know all of you can help me.

B: *[Nods]*

C: Mmm.

D: Okay.

From the start, it is made clear that the aim of the group is to help
the lead person make the target child happier in school. The easiest
and most accurate way of explaining the selection of members of the
group without prejudice, is to say they have been chosen because they
can all help.

E: He's being picked on!

L: Okay, I see ... I wonder if ever any of you have ever been
unhappy in school for any reason?

B: I was unhappy last year for a bit.

L: Oh, what was making you unhappy?

B: I was getting called names ...

L: I see ... I can understand that would make you feel
unhappy; I hope you are okay now in school, are you?

B: Yes

L: Good – we want everyone to be happy coming to our
school, don't we? That's why I want your help. Will you
help me?

B: Yeah.

D: Sure!

A: Mmm ... *[Others nodding]*

E: What do you want us to do?

L: I thought I would be able to count on all of you to help me.

Occasionally, even though they have not been asked, a child may offer
an explanation as to why the child is unhappy. If so, a brief acknowl-

edgement can be made before moving on. As an example, the group can be asked if any of them have ever been unhappy in school. If so, they usually relate similar circumstances which seem to show an implicit knowledge of the situation. However, the intervention is not dependent on the group feeling empathy with the victim and none of the group is assumed to lack it. They are being asked to do something to help the member of staff, regardless of any feelings they may have for the pupil. Most children want to help adults in school, so when the intervention is presented in this way, even if they are not particularly concerned about this child, they are more than likely to want to fulfil the request.

> L: You know Sam best, I am sure you can think of ideas that might help. Has anyone got a suggestion, maybe just a small thing you can do sometime over the next week that will make him happier in school?
>
> A: I could talk to him, if he's on his own …
>
> L: That's a very good idea – you were quick to think of that – I'm sure that would help. So, Amed … *[writing it down]* talk to him if he's alone … thank you. That's great – just the sort of help I'm wanting. Who else has got an idea?
>
> B: I could sit with him at lunchtimes.
>
> L: I'm sure that would help too, another great idea! Ben … *[writing it down]* sit with him at lunchtime. You will be able to remember to do that, will you?
>
> B: Yeah, I have a packed lunch like he does.
>
> L: That's great! Who else has got an idea – it doesn't need to be anything too big …
>
> C: I can tell him some jokes.
>
> L: That's a lovely idea, Carl – do you know some jokes that will make him laugh?
>
> C: Yeah, I know some good jokes.
>
> L: You are good at telling jokes, are you? That's excellent!
>
> D: I can bring him some sweets!
>
> L: That's very kind of you to do that … So Carl will tell him some jokes and Danny is going to share some of his sweets … *[writing the suggestions down]*

Some groups are full of ideas immediately whilst others are at first not so forthcoming. Once a couple of group members have made suggestions that have been positively received, the others are usually keen to pitch in with their own. Every suggestion is welcomed and they can be complimented for it, unless it is clearly unacceptable.

Their suggestions are reinforced by writing down their names and repeating their exact words, being curious about what they are going to do and admiring their kindness or bright ideas. This demonstrates to the whole group that making a suggestion gains approval. The list is not intended to be used to check that they have done whatever they suggested during the next meeting.

The examples given here are typical suggestions from children in primary school. Their significance lies in the fact that they show the pupils are willing to take part and accept the aim of the group to help make the target child happier. Some are brilliant. One of the best I had was, *I'll watch for him coming through the gate in the morning and smile and say, hello!*

Sometimes there may be one or two children who cannot think of anything else for them to do. They can be invited to help another member of the group or be given more time to think about it.

E: I can't think of anything.

L: That's okay, maybe you will think of something later, or perhaps you can help one of the others doing something?

E: I could sit with him at lunchtime, too.

F: I can play with him at playtime.

L: I'm sure both those will be very helpful, thank you …
These are all great ideas I have down here – I'm sure they will help Sam become happier – well done for thinking of all these ideas!

F: Do you want us to tell you if anybody picks on him?

L: Thank you, but I'm hoping there will be no need … if you manage to do all these brilliant ideas, it will be great!

It is essential that the pupils, rather than the lead person, make the suggestions and choose what to do themselves, so the resulting plan truly belongs to the group. The lead person may need to resist a temptation to give the group members 'jobs', or make them promise to do anything, or ask them to be friends with the target pupil.

Once all the members of the group have a part to play in the plan, the suggestions can be summarized, repeating their words again, together with their names.

> L: I'm so pleased you are all going to help me with this: Amed by talking to Sam; Ben and Ethan by sitting with him at lunchtimes; Carl, telling him some jokes; Danny bringing him some sweets and Freddie playing with him at playtime. It looks to me like you have managed to come up with a really good plan. I am sure the group will be successful and Sam will be happier in school over the next week because of all these things you will be doing. You have all been very helpful - thank you so much.
>
> I would like to know how you are getting on – may I see you all again in a week's time, so you can let me know what you have managed to do? [*group nodding*] Okay, next Wednesday, I'll send for you. I'll look forward to that. Good luck! I'm sure your ideas will help Sam feel a lot happier.

Their plan can be complimented by sounding optimistic about the chances of success, repeating the aim of the group and thanking them in anticipation for their help.

By this point in the meeting the support group is usually keen on the idea of reporting back to the lead person about what they have done. A week is usually a suitable length of time before the next meeting, so that they have all had a chance to do something and any initial 'over-enthusiasm' has settled down.

## Review with the child being supported

About a week after establishing the group, the situation can be reviewed, initially with the child being supported. This is often a very short meeting since everything is usually going fine and the pupil is often by now happy in school. The child's role in any improvements should be recognized – after all, they too will have made changes and it is helpful if their own contribution to the solution is acknowledged and emphasised.

> L: How are things now?
> S: Fine!
> L: That's great! What's been better?
> S: Carl has been talking to me at lunchtime.
> L: Oh, so you have been talking with Carl?
> S: Yes, and with Amed.
> L: So you're managing to talk with others more now, that's good, well done. What else have you been doing that's better?
>
> L: Do you think you will be fine now or would you like me to see you again in a week or so?
> S: I'll be fine.
> L: Well done, I'm impressed how you've managed to sort it out so quickly.

If there are any doubts at all, another meeting can be arranged. If the child is confident enough to carry on alone, they can be praised for this, too. Although it will always be a matter of judgment, the support given should be sufficient but no more than necessary to solve the problem, in order to avoid any kind of dependency.

## Review with the support group

Enough time needs to be allowed in this review so that each member of the group has the opportunity to talk about whatever it is they have done and to be complimented individually. There is no need to check whether they did the things they suggested the week before – that is not important – and there is no need for everyone to be required to say what they have done.

> L: Right, it's good to see you again, how are things going?
> A: He's okay, now!
> L: Good, that's great! What a brilliant group! So, how did you manage to help?

B: I've been playing football with him at breaktime.

L: Have you? That's no doubt helped him feel happier, do you think?

B: Yes.

L: Well done! What else has anyone done to help?

C: I've been calling for him on the way to school.

L: What a great idea – it's kind of you to think of that. Do you think that's helped?

C: Yes, he is happier now. He said so.

L: That's brilliant! Anyone else?

E: Somebody was calling him names at lunchtime, but I told him to leave him alone.

L: And did that help?

E: Yes, he's stopped doing it.

L: Well done, thanks for sorting that out so sensibly. What else makes you think he is happier now?

F: We've been talking to him at lunchtime, too.

L: Oh, I'm guessing he would enjoy that ... Well, I must say, I am impressed by the way you have been helping. Well done all of you! It sounds like this group has been really successful ... How would you like to continue for another week?

A: Yeah, sure!

B: I'll do it for as long as you like!

L: That will be great. I'll send for you again in a week and you can let me know what you have been doing ... Good luck again, bye!

Sometimes one or two pupils in the group stay quiet during this first review. Maybe they have not done anything, or perhaps they have just stopped doing something that made the other child unhappy. They can still be included in the praise for the success of the group as a whole.

Occasionally, one of them may report that there has been some difficulty, most often from someone not in the group. This might not have been mentioned, perhaps not even noticed, by the child being supported. Someone in the support group often takes the initiative and sorts out anything minor like this. After all, some of these children may be influential in their wider peer group.

The group as a whole is congratulated for a job well done. If there is any doubt at all, they can be asked if they would like to continue for another week. They can be very enthusiastic about this – after all, they have not been tasked with anything too onerous, or anything they did not themselves offer to do. Most frequently, the situation will be reviewed twice, just to ensure that the pattern of interaction has changed. In a minority of cases it may need reinforcing for up to five reviews. It is very rare to go beyond this number. Also, the time between reviews can be gradually increased.

(An example format for recording an intervention is included as Appendix A.)

### 'Jenny'

The mother of an eight-year-old girl, Jenny, phoned the local education authority to complain about her daughter being bullied at school. I made a visit to the home and Jenny's mother, Mrs Brown, told me that her daughter had been bullied in school from the start but it had become particularly worrying during the past 18 months. She had been into school and spoken to both the headteacher and Jenny's class teacher on several occasions. Recently, Mrs Brown had felt guilty sending Jenny into school because she had begun to be tearful in the mornings. Jenny had retaliated once and hit another child who was teasing her on the way home from school. Although Mrs Brown had sympathy for this child, she felt justified in insisting that the bullying of Jenny had to stop. Other children had been hiding her things in class, taking away her chair as she was sitting down and pulling her hair.

I went into school immediately after seeing Mrs Brown. The headteacher was annoyed that she had contacted the education office, since they had been doing their best in school to rectify the situation. He thought that she was over-anxious and Jenny was being 'spoiled'. He was dealing with it properly and nothing more could be done. I arranged to see Jenny and return the following week.

Although her mother had mentioned a few girls as being instrumental, Jenny herself said one boy was difficult for her in the playground. There were three other girls who were usually around. She named two girls as her friends.

During the next visit, the headteacher said he would be happy for me to make any suggestions. I spoke to the class teacher who was concerned that Jenny was 'the most sensitive girl she had come across in all her years of teaching'; she was often tearful, could not take any kind of criticism and any problems the teacher investigated frequently came to nothing. She considered Jenny's behaviour was attention-seeking; she had no real friends and generally played on her own outside.

On this occasion, I suggested the teacher led a support group. When I called again in two weeks' time Jenny told me the girls had been playing with her. I also saw the support group and they thought she was fine now. When I phoned her mother, she agreed things were better, although one day Jenny had been slapped in the face by another girl. She did not know if this girl was a member of the support group. I arranged to visit again a week later.

At the next meeting, Jenny said things were still going well. The group thought that Jenny was happy now in school. When I phoned her mother for her impressions, she was very pleased. She had been to a parents' evening that week and received a good report from Jenny's teacher. She felt 'her confidence had grown in leaps and bounds' and she was happy for me to close the referral. The teacher arranged for them all, including Jenny, to receive certificates in assembly.

This case was unusual insofar as I encouraged the teacher to lead the group, mainly because it appeared the school was uncomfortable that someone from outside had been called in to help when they felt they had been responding appropriately. Although this meant there was a slight delay in setting up the group, I did not want to undermine the school's determination to deal with the problem and in return they were happy to try a new strategy. There was only the one incident, reported by her mother, during the first week. From referral to closure took just over four weeks.

Even when different people have contradictory ideas about what is happening, it is still possible to accept whatever is said and move on without needing to find out what the 'truth' is. Once the child is again happy in school, none of the details of the problem past matter so much anyway.

## The effectiveness of support groups

After the supported pupil is once again happy in school, all the group members are positive in the reviews and the parent is satisfied that there is no longer any bullying, the intervention is finished. The most important outcome is that the child is happy at school. The success of using a support group in primary schools, at first beyond all expectations, led to a review and publication of the results of the referrals where a support group had been used (Young, 1998).

Usually referrals came to the local authority anti-bullying project from parents, although increasingly schools themselves requested help. Up to that point solution-focused support groups as described above had been tried and completed in 50 cases. It was found that bullying had ceased in 47 of these 50 cases (94%) and in 40 of those the bullying stopped immediately the group was set up. In the seven others the support group had continued to meet for up to five reviews before the intervention was considered to be completely successful. In the three cases where there remained ongoing difficulties, the situation had at least improved – in none of the cases did any bullying grow worse.

When evaluating the support group strategy, the most astonishing finding was the speed of effect. Setting up a support group stopped any bullying immediately in 80% of cases and in less than six weeks in 94% of cases. Not only was the strategy effective for the great majority of referrals, it also proved fast acting.

What is more, using a support group to stop bullying has a long-term effect. Bullying only seemed to recur in a very small minority of referrals, usually by pupils who were not in the original group. Staff working in schools and leading support groups, arguably in a better position to judge the longer-term effectiveness, also found this to be the case. The principles of conflict resolution tell us that a win-win outcome is the best option, not least because it is more likely to provide a lasting solution. It is perhaps not surprising that the support group strategy, where all the pupils involved are winners, proves to be sustainable over the longer term.

Leading support groups is a strategy that is accessible to school staff. Numerous people in schools have tried it successfully and, importantly, at the first attempt. In one school that decided to use this approach on a regular basis, I was allowed to see the impressive records kept by a teaching assistant over a large number of referrals, and they pointed to an even higher success rate.

De Shazer (1985) used a metaphor about keys to describe a characteristic of solution-focused strategies. Skeleton keys work in many different locks. In the same way as skeleton keys do not match the complexity of individual locks – they only need to fit – so solution-focused strategies are not as complicated as each problem they solve. The support group approach works like a skeleton key. It unlocks the solution even though there may be limitless differences between individual referrals. A solution key does not have to match the problem precisely. For it to be a solution, it has only to work.

**Pupils as partners**
Pupils respond very positively to being asked to participate in a group. When they are put in the position of helping a member of staff, they value it as a sign of trust and responsibility. The teaching assistant mentioned above had the advantage of time set aside to run support groups because there were serious concerns about children's safety at the school following an inspection. Pupils became so familiar and comfortable with the strategy that they would approach the assistant when they wanted to set up a group for another child. Rather than 'telling' about bullying, they were 'telling' about who needed support. She noticed a gradual reduction in the seriousness of the cases that she dealt with and she put this down to children being more likely to ask for help earlier. Support groups had enabled pupils to become partners in anti-bullying.

It is understandably hard to believe on the face of it that anyone who is bullying someone else would change their behaviour so quickly. This intervention was not based on any theory, but there is plenty of research that can explain, in retrospect, why it works so well. It could be said the theory is irrelevant so long as the strategy works, but there is an understandable desire to act in accordance with rational explanations rather than relying on received wisdom or just 'magic'.

Researchers in social psychology have studied the responses of 'bystanders' and identified factors likely to promote helpful behaviour (Brewer & Crano, 1994; Deaux et al., 1993; Baron et al., 1992; in

Young, 1998). The same conditions are present for all members of a support group. They all:
- have agreed to help
- know that help is needed
- have been given responsibility
- have been assigned a specific task

Additionally, working as part of a group further enhances the chances of individual members being helpful because:
- their suggestions have been accepted by the group
- even if only one member of a group acts initially, other members are likely to follow
- their commitment is 'public'
- belonging to a successful group increases self-esteem
- unhelpful behaviour is unacceptable to the rest of the group
- interdependence encourages mutually beneficial behaviour
- the group are rewarded with appreciation for their success

Traditionally the aim of bullying has been understood and indeed defined as a 'bully' exerting power unfairly over a weaker 'victim'. Since the bully is always more powerful, it is fair to assume that the aim of bullying behaviour is not to gain status over the victim. In school bullying, there are almost always other pupils around at the time. The frequency of their presence suggests they play an important role. If we consider it as being 'socially-situated', then bullying in school may be understood as a means of establishing and reinforcing status not over the victim *but over bystanders.*

When bullying is happening, the others around may be 'chosen' as carefully as the victim. Bullying will not happen if more powerful pupils who disapprove are present. Other pupils generally do not intervene when someone is being bullied; when they do, they may support what is going on. Their inaction or support allows the bullying to happen and implicitly reinforces the higher status of the bully. Generally bullying takes place within peer groups between pupils in the same year group or class, where social status is constantly being reinforced or challenged. Bullying, albeit unacceptable, is an efficient and relatively non-risky way of establishing or maintaining a pupil's status. When bullying or witnessing bullying, some pupils may not fully realise the distress that is being caused to the victim because their attention is focused on each others' reactions (see also Samilvalli, 1999).

When a support group is set up, the common aim is to make the target child happy in school. Clearly, if any bullying continues, the group is likely to fail. Anyone whose behaviour has been making the supported child unhappy for any reason will need to choose whether to continue as before or help make the group successful. An alternative means of achieving status is provided by taking a major role in the group's success. In this positive form we might even call it leadership.

Bullies, victims and bystanders are all to some extent trapped in a pattern of behaviour in any particular time and place. Providing a context and expectation of change is powerful in making it happen, to everyone's benefit. Because bystanders are such an important feature in school bullying they are able to play an equally important part in the solution. Whatever explanatory theories may be adopted, they are merely working assumptions; they are most helpful when they appreciate students' abilities to bring about change.

## The pupils' perspective

Although it would be very useful to have a video of a support group in action, this would inevitably cause delay whilst appropriate permission from parents was gained and it would raise a number of other ethical issues. Children have been interviewed in hindsight about their experiences of having been in support groups. All the groups to which they belonged had been led by a member of staff in the school. Six children from different support groups were interviewed, one of whom had been in three different groups. Even though pupils always appeared to gain from taking part in a support group, it was surprising just how positively they viewed the experience, both for the supported child and for themselves.

They all thought their groups had been successful in helping make the supported pupil happy in school. When asked how they knew this, there were various answers:

- Because after about two weeks she started making more friends ... She's made more friends and she plays with them.

- One time, I was playing with her and she just came … she was with me and she asked me if she could go and play with her other friends. And I said, 'Yeah, sure!' and I was really pleased for her because now she's got more friends to play with.
- He keeps coming to school … I'm in his class. He comes nearly every day now.
- He's improved in his work … and a lot of things … before in literacy he wasn't doing very good … 'cos [he] was in bottom group but now he's in middle [group].
- At playtimes, the girl who felt real sad … she was happier. She was smiling and laughing.
- Yeah, she's really happy … she walks past me, I ask her how she's doing, and she says 'Hello'.

They were asked how they felt about being in the support group:
- In the support groups, everybody like … inside, you feel real sorry for somebody and … you feel like you don't have to do it to other people, 'cos it's not very nice and you wouldn't like it, if it was you.
- I felt like I'd done a good job.
- It felt like I was making more friends with her.
- I felt happier when I helped the other person feel happier as well.
- I liked the meetings – it made me feel important.

Solution-focused support groups had given these children the opportunity of responding in a helpful way to their peers which, quite rightly, made them feel good about themselves too.

(Thanks to the staff and children who helped make the video at The Parks Primary School, Hull.)

**Including parents as partners**
Often the complaint about bullying will come from a parent, who will be told that a group of other children will be asked to help, and that the group may include as well as friends, pupils that their child has found difficult. They can be reassured that in most cases this strategy works very quickly and they should notice an improvement soon. Parents are also reassured when contact is maintained and they are asked for their views on how the situation is improving during the intervention. After

all, they know their child best and their input can help staff judge when the child is happy in school and the group has been effective.

If the person leading the group is from outside the school, permission from parents of children in the group may be necessary, depending on school policy. If permission is needed, there would need to be a conversation along the lines of:

*We are setting up a small group to help another child in school at the moment. We would like your son/daughter to be part of it because we think s/he can help. The children enjoy this kind of responsibility. It may last three or four weeks. We would like you to know, so that if they should mention it at home, you can encourage what s/he is doing. Thank you.*

If peer support is part of the normal practice in school – to encourage a friendly and supportive community – and if the leader of the group is a member of the school staff, which would be preferable, then there is no need to inform parents.

Once the group is successful, some schools give certificates to the group members or take a photograph of everyone together. A few parents have framed these and put them up on their walls and some schools include them in displays to promote their caring ethos. Whereas complaints about bullying can put a strain on a school's relationships with parents (and between parents), this approach maintains and enhances a cooperative alliance.

## Secondary schools

Teachers have often asked if peer support groups work in secondary schools. There were only a few support groups that had been set up in secondary schools at the time of the review of referrals mentioned above. These were disregarded in the evaluation because they did not constitute a sufficiently large sample from which to draw reliable conclusions. Generally speaking, however, pastoral staff in secondary schools have preferred to lead support groups themselves and when they have given feedback, they reported the intervention was successful.

## A girl in secondary school

The parents of a 14-year-old girl, Petra, were anxious to know what could be done to support their daughter. They said she was heavily built, although not obese, and she was no longer participating in any sport that required her to get changed. Other students had apparently been teasing her, particularly about her breasts. The parents had tried to allay her embarrassment and had even taken her to the doctor to discuss it. The teacher had initially been sympathetic but had, as the parents saw it, lost patience with their daughter and blamed her for allowing the teasing to bother her. The parents described her as sensitive and sometimes seemingly a 'bit of a loner'.

When I saw Petra in school, she gave the names of two girls in her class who bothered her most, and four others who were usually around but, she said, 'didn't start anything themselves'. She also gave the names of two girls who were her friends.

The support group consisted of all these students and was seen immediately, without Petra present. A teacher from the school, as usual, was invited to sit in the session. The students seemed suspicious of my involvement at first. I said nothing about Petra's anxieties. Their suggestions included sitting with her in certain classes – no-one mentioned PE – and chatting with her at break times. One member of the group mentioned that she often went off the school site at lunchtimes, which was not allowed without permission. A couple of the girls said they would 'leave her alone' when she annoyed them.

When Petra was seen again in school a week later, she said things were a lot better – and she was intending to participate in a games lesson for the first time that term. She felt confident enough because she had not been teased since the support group had been set up and the teacher had reassured her that she would watch out for her.

When I saw the group, they were fairly quiet again at first. A couple of students were missing because of an after-school commitment elsewhere. One of the girls said Petra was 'okay now'. They agreed she had been chatting more and had stayed in school a couple of times at lunch. Two of the girls said they had told her she could count on their friendship. They were all happy to continue being supportive. When I complimented them on their success, they gave the impression that they thought it was a minor problem.

I contacted her parents by phone. They were delighted that Petra seemed much less anxious, and was even talking about school quite happily – which they said had not happened for a long time. They expressed their complete surprise that there had been this improvement and admitted they had not really been confident that anything would change, let alone so quickly.

Despite having some success, there remain some reservations about using support groups in secondary schools, even when led by a member of staff inside the school. Occasionally teenage students are adamant that they do not want anything to happen that involves speaking to anyone else at all. As students become older, they increasingly need to be consulted and give informed consent to any intervention, whatever that may be. Often resistance can be taken as a sign that the situation needs to be dealt with differently.

Referrals for bullying from secondary schools can be of a very serious nature. For example, in one case a teenage girl had been sexually assaulted and in another someone had been threatened with a knife. In these instances the police were involved. A peer support group would not be recommended in these situations, or at least not a group including anyone under investigation.

The next chapter describes solution-focused interviewing for working with an individual student who is feeling troubled. Where a support group has not been appropriate for any reason, particularly in secondary schools, this type of individual intervention has been proven to be very effective.

## Summary

School staff deal successfully with incidents of bullying on a day-to-day basis but difficulties can arise when it is not entirely clear what is happening. Even when it is obvious, often teachers do not want to risk making matters worse by causing any resentment from dealing with it 'head on'.

Solution-focused peer support groups concentrate attention on the preferred future, leaving any difficulties behind. Pupils' knowledge of their lives in school makes even young children skilled at knowing the small but significant actions they can take to help make another child happy in school, and they value the opportunity to do so.

In secondary schools there may be circumstances that preclude the use of peer group support, and where it is not possible, individual solution-focused conversations have been shown to be effective. The next chapter describes this type of intervention.

# Chapter 6
# Individual Interviewing

## Introduction

Chapter 1 outlined the principal features of solution-focused practice identified by de Shazer and his team while working with clients and families. This chapter illustrates those features with examples of dialogue taken from the context of supporting a pupil who is experiencing difficulties with bullying in school. This is followed by the outcomes that were achieved following this type of intervention, in an anti-bullying project that routinely used solution-focused interviews; and finally there are recommendations for further reading.

## Solution-focused conversation

In a skilled solution-focused conversation all the questions asked and any comments the interviewer makes are disciplined and purposeful. The interviewer's skill lies in formulating series of questions, often building closely on previous answers, to identify and connect the interviewee's successful past with their preferred future. The most important assumptions throughout the interview are that the student is the expert on their own life, and that they have all the strengths and personal qualities they need to make their life more like they want it to be in school. The craft of the interviewer is to enable this expertise to come to the fore and to inform the interviewee about small but significant changes that will help bring it about. Several types of questions are commonly used that have been found to be particularly helpful. Over the following pages examples are given using excerpts from typical solution-focused conversations, taken from first, subsequent and final sessions.

## Getting Started

It is useful to begin by engaging the student in some 'non-problem' talk that is light and positive. This conveys the message that the interviewer is more interested in the pupil than the problem and assumes there are areas of the pupil's life that are free of difficulties, as indeed there will be. A deliberate focus on areas of competence is useful, because the interviewer will be listening for possible strengths and resources right from the outset. Asking routine questions that they will be able to answer easily also helps to build a cooperative mindset and allay the pupil's nervousness.

INTERVIEWER: Hi there! What have you been doing while it's been raining over the week-end?

STUDENT: Nothing much.

I: Nothing much, eh? … What were you doing mostly?

S: Just watching TV.

I: What do you like watching?

S: Football.

I: Do you support any team in particular?

S: Manchester …

I: Oh, Manchester, eh? How are they doing at the moment?

S: Yeah … okay.

I: Can I just check on a few things? You're in year 8 I think?

S: *[Nods]*

I: And your tutor is …?

S: Mr Smith.

I: Ah yes … thank you … Mr Smith *[writing it down]* I'll just be making a few notes of things I think may be important, that I don't want to forget … okay?

S: *[Nods]*

Some prefer not to make notes during an interview but writing down a few details can be a helpful reminder about successes and strengths that might be raised again later. Note-taking is also a silent demonstration of what the listener thinks is important – so apart from administrative details such as name and teacher, writing can be used to accentuate any interests, areas of competence, strategies that have worked in the past or times when the problem does not occur or is happening less. It helps if the notes are visible to the pupil. Most of the dialogue from the interviewer will be in the form of questions. The student is unlikely to expect these kinds of questions, so it is important to go slowly, giving students plenty of time to consider them before answering.

I: So ... what are you good at in school?

S: Err ... football ... and art.

I: Of course, football ... and art ... What have you been doing recently that you've enjoyed in art?

S: We've been doing some drawing ...

I: Ah ... so you enjoy drawing? What have you drawn recently that you were pleased with?

*What are you good at?* is a great question to start with. As so often in solution-focused interviewing, this question deliberately makes an appreciative assumption – that there is something that the student is good at. (Contrast the similar question and yet different assumption behind: *Are you good at anything?* which almost invites *no* for an answer.) The question reminds the student of times when life is better, probably times when the problem is absent, or perhaps less troublesome. These are all areas the interviewer can explore further, or make a note to return to later.

I: Right, so I understand from Mr Smith that he thinks things are not too happy for you at the moment in school? Is that right?

S: Mmm.

I: I want to help – is that okay with you?

S: Yeah.

I: Right, I will be asking a lot of questions. I want to find out more about what you're good at and what will be happening when things are going better for you ... okay?

S: Hmm, yeah ...

It often seems natural to check out how the interview came about, since young people in school have not usually requested to be seen.

It is helpful to 'externalise' any problem mentioned, in this case by using terms such as 'things are not too happy' rather than 'you are not happy' and limiting the time-scale with 'at the moment'. Without assuming what is causing the problem, it is respectful to ask permission to proceed – putting oneself in the position of cooperating with the student, especially since the general rule in school is that students are expected to cooperate with staff.

## Aims

It is important early in the interview to formulate a goal, or at least a direction in terms of the student's preferred future. Even though at this stage it may be fairly vague, having an aim in mind is important or it will be difficult to judge if the sessions have really been effective in bringing about any desired change. This can be used as a 'touchstone' throughout the first and any future sessions, or amended as appropriate. De Shazer thought that the lack of working towards a clear goal was the most common reason for failure. More details about the preferred future will emerge as the conversation unfolds, and it will be returned to again later. It is easy to assume that we already know what the student wants, but only they can really know how they want their life to be in school and how they will recognize when they get there. This is one of the ways the interviewee is acknowledged and encouraged to be the expert in their own lives.

I: How would you like things to be better?

S: I'm getting bullied … I'd like them to stop bullying me.

I: Yes, of course, that must be difficult … and when they stop … what difference will that make to you in school?

S: They won't be bullying me … I'd be happier …

I: Happier, yes, I can understand that … so what will you be doing different, when you are happier?

S: I'd be able to get on with my work …

I: Oh right … so when you are happier, how will you be able to get on with your work more?

S: I'll be able to concentrate on my work … get it finished.

I: I see … Which lesson will you notice this in first – able to be happy and concentrate on your work?

Often the desire may be for an absence of something, such as bullying, which may lie outside their direct control. If so, the description needs to be about what will be happening instead. It is more helpful to the student if the focus is on actions within their control. In this case, the student is encouraged to describe how being happier will affect how he behaves.

**Scaling**
Scaling is used frequently in solution-focused practice. As shown in previous chapters, it clarifies the present position and provides a baseline from which progress can be measured by the student in future sessions and overall. The lowest parameter should reflect a position below where the pupil is at present and 10 will relate to the aim of the session being achieved. (I prefer to use 1 rather than 0, the assumption being that there is always something to build on.)

    I: So we have an idea of where it is at the moment … on a scale of 1 to 10 *[drawing a line across a paper marking it with a 1 and 10 at each end, allowing the student to look and point, if they wish]* 1 is the worst you can imagine it getting – the pits. 10 is when you are happy in school and able to get on with your work. Where would you say it is now?
    S: Around the middle – 4 or 5.
    I: Shall we say … a definite 4, then? *[marking the point on the line]*
    S: Yeah.

The 10 should be realistic rather than aspirational (e.g. not *the happiest you've ever been*) and 1 should denote below how things stand at present. Using a phrase like *the worst you can imagine it getting* implies 1 is below where it is at the moment. Being careful how the 1 and the 10 are defined helps the student construct the present position somewhere in between, ideally towards the middle. (If nevertheless the student scales it at 0 or 1, it would be better to continue with 'coping questions', see further below.) Some students find it helpful to have an actual line drawn on paper that they can examine closely as they think of their answers to scaling questions. They can place the mark on the line for themselves and then decide what the number should be. First of all, scaling provides a powerful way of getting the conversation to concentrate on the past or present experiences where there is less of a problem.

## Successful past

Immediately after scaling, the next question is always along the lines of, *What makes it so high?* The position chosen on the scale usually indicates that they do experience at least a few relatively positive times which can then be explored, with the interviewer maintaining taking a curious stance and asking for more and more details.

I: About a 4 … that's good … What are you doing already that is making it a 4 … and not, say, a 3?

S: Well … I do have one or two friends …

I: Oh, that's great, who are they?

S: Jackson and Curtis.

I: What do you like doing with your friends, Jackson and Curtis?

S: Playing football.

I: Oh yes … when do you get the chance to play football with them?

S: At break or at lunchtimes, sometimes.

I: So you like playing football at break and lunchtimes? What do you like about Curtis that makes him a good choice for a friend?

S: Well, playing football … and he talks to me, sometimes we hang out together after school …

Questions often build on the student's previous answers, repeating their own words in the next question. These words are the most meaningful to the student and it is respectful to use the student's own language rather than rephrasing what has been said. In this case − having a couple of friends, playing football, hanging out after school − these ideas suggest possible, positive pathways to follow and explore further. When they are talking about these times, these exceptions maybe, their descriptions will imply evidence of skills and strengths, personal resources that thay can draw on to reach higher on their scale.

'Other person perspective' questions are very useful in eliciting more strengths and qualities, once the student has mentioned someone who appears to have a positive relationship with them. Questions from another person's point of view provides an indirect way of complimenting these qualities, and thereby bringing them to the front of the interviewee's mind, in some sense making them more available in the future.

I: I'm wondering ... if I were to ask Curtis what he likes about you – what he likes about having you as a friend – what would he say?

S: Probably the same ... playing football, talking together, having a laugh.

I: So you have a laugh with Curtis sometimes, do you? He likes that about you?

S: Yeah ... sometimes.

I: That's great ... So having these good friends and having a laugh helps you be at a 4 at the moment? What else are you managing to do, to make it a 4 and not a 3 or 2?

Concentrating attention on what the student is doing and what is happening generally during the periods when things are going better for them, reinforces that experience, making it more likely that they will do it more often. It also provides information that may be useful for them later in the interview when they are building a picture of what they will be doing in their preferred future. When a particular line of enquiry has been explored, a new one can be opened up by going back to the scale and asking 'what else' makes their position on the scale as high as it is.

In schools, students often have someone they can turn to when they have a problem. Notice in this example below, the student is not asked what he has talked about – it would probably lead to a description of the problem – but rather what it was about the talking that was useful.

I: What else helps make it a 4?

S: I tell Mrs Lloyd about what's been happening ... when I've been picked on.

I: Ah right, good, so how does that help?

S: Just being able to talk to someone – she says I can talk to her when I like … she's nice …

I: Being able to talk to her when you like … it certainly sounds like she cares about you … I wonder what tells her you're worth that time?

S: I don't know … I think she's pleased when things are better for me.

I: Yes … I'm sure. Can you give me an example when she has been pleased … when things were better for you?

S: She was pleased when I got a certificate for maths.

I: Oh right! You got a certificate in maths – that's excellent! What was that for doing in maths exactly?

S: For finishing all my work quickly, before anyone else …

I: Really? Well done! How did you manage to do that work so quickly?

S: I just got on with it … just got my head down and did it!

I: Wow! Good for you! It sounds like once you decide to do something you have the determination to do it?

As here, putting a compliment in the form of a question can make it easier to accept. When a pupil is struggling in school, their time and attention can be drained away from talking about achievements, out of concern for their difficulties. Solution-focused conversations redress this balance by amplifying the significance of any positive experiences.

Whatever the area of success, useful strengths and personal qualities can be noticed that may later be applied to areas of the preferred future. In this example, determination is a very useful quality to draw attention to. Towards the end of the session it can be mentioned again, linked to any suggestions that may be made.

Since wherever students place themselves on the scale is to some extent 'average', another tack that can be helpful is asking about what is happening at the times when it is higher. Although logically this is the same as asking what is making it where it is now, the different form of question can enable different answers to emerge.

I: I guess that since you are a 4 overall – there are times when you are more than 4? What's different about you at those times?

S: Yeah ... sometimes ... sometimes it's okay ... when I'm with my friends ... when they are leaving me alone ...

I: Yeah ... so when they are leaving you alone ... what sort of things are you doing at these times?

S: Well it's usually when I'm playing football with my friends, or when I'm getting on with my work ... ignoring them.

I: Oh! ... so you manage to ignore them sometimes?

S: Yeah ...

I: That can't be easy ... How do you manage to do that?

S: I just pay no attention ... I concentrate on what I am doing ... like I don't hear them.

I: So ... paying them no attention, concentrating on what you're doing, not hearing them ... all those things can be helpful?

S: Yeah ...

I: What else do you manage to do that helps?

S: Talk to my friends ...

The student should be encouraged to articulate exactly what they are doing when things are better, even though it might not appear at first to rely on anything the student has done, or at least not deliberately. It is particularly useful if they are describing something they are doing when the problem could be happening but is not. Often students say that they do not get bullied so much when they are with their friends, or when they are concentrating on their work. They may never have had the chance to contemplate this before and it draws attention to possible strategies that sometimes work and that they can use deliberately in the future. Reinforcing their effective action and appreciating their own resourcefulness are more powerful than giving advice that the interviewer thinks would be useful. Once the successful past has been explored in this way, it provides a 'springboard' to describe what they want to be happening in the future.

## A very brief encounter

Solution-focused conversations do not have to be long. Scaling provides a summary about where pupils are, without their having to explain any reasons why. One day as I was signing myself into a primary school, a girl I had worked with a few months earlier surprised me by sidling up and saying:

  C: Hello! … I'm an eight now!

 SY: An eight! How have you managed that?

  C: I've been working hard.

 SY: Excellent! Well done you! *[she continued on her way down the corridor with a smile and a wave goodbye!]*

It is touching when young people say thank-you for any help given to make them happy in school; but working in a solution-focused way there is an even better reward: their self-confidence from knowing they did it all themselves.

## Coping

Occasionally a student may say they are just a 1 on the scale, or in a subsequent session, less on the scale than the time before. An acknowledgement of the difficulties needs to be made before moving forward, although there is no need to ask about how they feel or what happened to make it so low. Asking about coping is very useful in this situation, because it implies resourcefulness and draws their attention to strategies that might be useful in the future.

  I: … Where would you say you are now on the scale?

  S: 1.

  I: Hmm! That must be difficult for you…

  S: It's terrible …

  I: Yes, I see … Hmm! How are you managing to cope with coming to school?

  S: I just try to ignore them.

  I: That can't be easy – how do you do that?

  S: I look away … I pretend I don't hear them … concentrate on what I'm doing …

I: Well done! … that must be hard sometimes. When you manage to concentrate on what you're doing, what difference does that make?

S: Sometimes they just give up …

I: If you pretend you just don't hear them?

S: Mrs Lloyd told me to just ignore them. She said they're just jealous.

I: Right, I can understand that … and when you manage to ignore them, what else do you do instead?

S: Err … I talked to my friends.

I: Ah, well done! … so when you talk to your friends … how does that help?

S: They said, 'Come on with us – let's get out of here …'

I: And that helped? That's excellent … well done you!

Any strategies the student uses that are helpful in difficult situations are worth exploring in detail. Students often mention 'ignoring'. Of course, it is difficult to simply ignore something that is hurtful, so it is helpful to ask what they do *when* they are ignoring – what are they paying attention to instead. Most strategies, such as ignoring, are sometimes helpful and sometimes not, so it is worth asking what exactly the student did or what were the circumstances when they used an idea successfully. This opens up the possibility of new actions, within their control, that they can deliberately adopt. As a general rule, whenever someone mentions that something they did not do was helpful, it is useful to ask what they did instead.

**Preferred future**

Although to some extent the preferred future has already been talked about in deciding the aim of the session, scaling provides a strategy for eliciting more helpful detail about the preferred future, typically by asking about what will be happening when the student is one notch further up on the scale. The question is not, *How will you get to a 5?* – a much better question is to ask for a description of what is different when it is a 5, or how will they know when they get there.

> I: Right, that's great … say I talk to you again in a week's time, and you say 'I'm a 5 now!' What will you be doing that tells you it's a 5?
> S: I'll be a bit happier …
> I: Yes, that's right, a bit happier … what will you be doing that's different from now when you are a bit happier, just a 5?
> S: I'll be talking to my friends more … Getting on with my work more, I suppose …
> I: Right, I see … tell me a bit more about talking to your friends … what will you be talking more about, do you think?
> S: Football … work … anything really …
> I: That's good … and getting on with your work more … what will tell you are managing to do that … enough to be a 5?
> S: I'll be finishing my work … getting more done …

Moving just one point up the scale is small yet significant progress and there are likely to be times when they have been there already. Maintaining a curious, 'not knowing' stance (De Jong & Berg, 2008) is central to solution-focused work. Although the interviewer may have their own ideas, the student is the only person who can answer questions like this with any authority, since the student is the only expert in their own life experience. In just the same way as before, each suggestion can be explored in detail, wondered about and enhanced, for as long as it is productive.

Another useful way of enabling a description of these differences is to use the idea of a video-recording.

> I: Good, yes! When you are happier, if there was a camera recording you … when it is a 5 … What will I see on the film that's different, that will tell me you're a five?
> S: I'll be talking to my mates … Smiling and having a laugh …
> I: You'll be smiling … that's great! Talking … and having a laugh … what else will I see?
> S: I'd be working more …

I: I see, really? How will I know that from watching the film?

S: I'll be writing ... or answering questions...

I: Ah! Answering questions – you will be answering more questions, will you?

S: Yeah.

I: How will you be managing to do that exactly?

S: I'll be listening to the teacher and thinking of the answers ...

I: So what will I see on the film that will tell me you are listening and thinking of the answers?

S: I'll be putting my hand up and answering.

As with other person perspectives, describing a video recording moves the description onto behaviour rather than feelings. Since behaviour and feelings are interactive – our feelings affect our actions and our actions affect our feelings – and there is a sense in which behaviour is more under personal control than feelings, it is more helpful to concentrate attention on the change in observable actions rather than emotions or thoughts. In just the same way as a teacher managing a class knows that looking at the teacher and sitting still actually helps pupils' attentiveness, any outward actions that belong to more positive thoughts and feelings are helpful for the student to recognize.

The more detailed and specific the description of the preferred future, the more likely the pupil will use it as a mental rehearsal for the actual future. With younger children, the interviewer can ask the child to act out their ideas there and then, e.g. *Can you show me now, what you do when you're listening well in class? ... Oh I see, you are sitting straight and looking forward ... staying still and quiet, that's excellent listening, well done!*

When asking solution-focused questions, it is not unusual for the first response to be, 'I don't know'. They are not necessarily easy to answer immediately and preferred future questions drift into the realm of speculation. Since anything imagined is based on what the student already knows, it is valuable as long as it is both optimistic and realistic. The student needs to be allowed enough time to think and allow for playfulness, guessing, wondering and imagining.

I: Great! ... And when you're a 5, who else will notice you're doing this ... putting your hand up ...?

S: The teacher might notice …

I: Really … you will be that good! … Which teacher will be the first to notice these changes in you in class?

S: Hmm … I don't know …

I: You can have a guess, maybe?

S: Mrs Smith, perhaps.

I: Hmm! What makes you think Mrs Smith may be the first to notice?

S: She often says something when people are working well.

I: Oh! That's nice! Can you remember a time when she's said something to you?

S: Yeah … she's said I did a good piece of work.

I: Excellent! A good piece of work, well done! What made it so good?

*Or/and* How did you manage that?

*Or/and* What difference did that make to you?

*Or/and* When you are a 5, who else will notice?

When watching a skilled interviewer, it seems as if they always know the best question to ask next. As in this example, choices are made about which path to follow and other questions could have been asked. When a choice is made, writing a note about any other option(s) can help remind an interviewer to return to this later, if they wish. The only way of knowing a good question is by listening to the answer (de Shazer, 1994).

**Miracle Question**

The miracle question is commonly used in solution-focused practice as a means of moving into a description of the preferred future, leaving the problem behind. A similar set of questions can be formed around imagining 'a good day'. Generally speaking, the effects of the miracle will be the same as being 10 on the scale, when life in school is how the student wants it to be.

It is not an easy question to ask well, and it is worth forewarning the student that an unusual question is coming up. It needs to be spoken slowly, setting the scene and checking for understanding as it unfolds.

I: I want to ask you a strange question! It's not an easy question to answer. You are great at answering my questions; you may have to think about this one! Okay?

S: Yeah.

I: Imagine the rest of today is just normal … it's a normal evening. You go to bed tonight and fall asleep. Okay?

S: Yeah.

I: And while you are sleeping … a miracle happens! The miracle is that you are happy in school, just like that! Tomorrow morning, when you wake up, you don't know this miracle has happened, because it happened while you were asleep, do you see?

I: Yeah.

S: So … the question is … tomorrow morning … what is the first thing you notice, tomorrow, that tells you this miracle has happened? What is different?

It is an intriguing question, inviting the student to visualise what life would actually be like the day after the miracle when the problem has vanished. Questions can deliberately be asked in the present tense, even though they are about the future, as in, *What is different?* instead of, *What will/would be different?* The effect of this is to encourage answers in the present tense too, giving any description more immediacy and force.

Using their own language, and focusing on the differences in how life appears the day after the miracle, the questions can be curious about any aspect the student mentions, gathering more and more detail, describing what happens on the 'miracle' day. The first thing mentioned may be the absence of the problem, but it is the effect this absence has on their day that is most helpful for them to imagine and predict.

I: What's the first thing you notice?

S: They're not bullying me.

I: That's right … so tomorrow … what is different about you?

S: I'm happy … I'm happy to go to school …

I: You're happy to go to school? What will tell you this?

S: I'll be smiling, getting ready to go to school …

I: I'm wondering ... who else will notice this miracle has happened?

S: I suppose my mum might notice ... she won't have to keep telling me to get ready ...

I: Oh right! That's good ... what is she saying then, instead?

S: I don't know ... 'You've got time for breakfast today!'

I: That's great ... so you're smiling, ready for school, and have time for breakfast. How will it be different, when you're having breakfast?

S: I'll be chatting with my mum ... maybe helping her make some toast ...

I: Helping your mum, eh? That sounds good to me! What else will she notice different when this miracle has happened?

S: I'll be happy to go to school ...

I: How will she know that?

S: She'll see I'm smiling and chatting.

I: What difference does this make to her?

S: She won't be so worried about what's going on at school.

I: Right, it's good for her too, then?

S: Yeah.

I: What happens next on this miracle day, tomorrow?

S: I'll meet up with friends and play football in the yard ...

I: Ah yes, you play football ... when you are playing football with your friends ... what is different about that, tomorrow, after the miracle?

S: We'll be having a laugh ...

As before, other people's perspectives can be useful to amplify the differences, as earlier in the interview. In this example, a new perspective is offered by the mention of a parent. The tiniest detail of any difference can be explored – what is different about getting up in the morning is a good example of eliciting small differences that can make all the difference (Shennan, 2003). The more detailed the description becomes, the more likely they will notice aspects of the miracle that are already happening or bits of the miracle they can enact in the near future.

## A miracle question

This question originated when a client of Insoo Kim Berg suggested a miracle would have to happen for their sessions together to be useful. Insoo continued by asking what would be different if a miracle did happen.

This fascinating question can enable clients to imagine and talk about what would be different in their life without the problem – the preferred future – without having to consider how it might come about. It can lead to surprising answers. I do not use this question routinely in my interviewing in schools; I tend to turn to it if I feel a bit stuck. In this case, I asked a boy aged 13, who had special needs, the miracle question in his fourth session. As happens occasionally, the student acted as if he were literally waking up, blinking and opening his eyes, looking around as if he was searching for what was different.

SY: ... So tomorrow morning ... what is the first thing you will notice that will tell you this miracle ... you are happy at school ... has happened?

B: *[Pause]* They won't be bullying me!

SY: That's right, you are happy at school. What is the first thing that you will notice different about you?

B: *[Long pause]* I'll know my alphabet ...

Although rather taken aback by this answer, it emerged that the alphabet was something he thought he should know and wanted to learn. When I continued to ask for more details ...

SY: What else will be different, after the miracle ... tomorrow ... when you are happy in school?

B: I'll be using my big voice ...

SY: Your big voice?

B: Yes, I have a big voice ...

SY: Really? That's interesting! May I hear your big voice ...?

B: It's like this! *[In his 'big' voice, clearer and stronger]*

SY: Wow, that's a good, big voice you have! *[Both laughing]*

At the end of this session I wrote the alphabet on a card for him. At our next session, he was clearly very proud to recite it from memory, in his big voice. He said he was pleased now he knew his alphabet and he had been using his big voice more. He had moved up one place on his scaling of being happier in school.

## Closing Phase

A solution-focused interview will typically end by reaffirming the aim or direction the student wants to take. The interviewer gives the student feedback by way of compliments about their personal qualities and use of resources that have helped in the past and will strengthen their ability to make progress. Any suggestions about possible next steps will be based on doing more of what works and be related to their description of the preferred future and the aim of the session.

I: Okay … That's great … I've asked a lot of questions and you have been excellent at answering them! I can understand that you want to be happier in school and to be able to get on with your work more, yeah?

S: Yes.

I: I am impressed by how – even when sometimes it's been difficult for you – you manage to still talk to your friends and play football with them. I'm also impressed with your determination, particularly when you are working in class.

S: *[Nods]*

I: I would like you to notice … when you are just a 5 on the scale … what else are you doing that's different? And I want you to remember for next time …

S: Mmm!

I: How about you have a go at that? How long to you think you need to give yourself time to do that?

S: About a week …

I: Okay, that's great! How about we arrange to meet up again in about a week so you can tell me what you've noticed?

It is not unusual to give a 'noticing task' in the first session. When someone is asked to notice something in particular, it is likely to happen more often, or at least they will be more aware of it happening than before. In this example, a suggestion could have been to continue playing football, or to talk to friends more often, or even to help make the toast. As with questions, the only way of knowing whether it was a good suggestion is in the next session, with the advantage of hindsight.

Finally, an arrangement to meet again can be made for when it will be most helpful to the student, usually when there's been enough time to experiment with any suggestion.

## Next session

Subsequent sessions follow very similar lines to the first. Following any brief non-problem talk at the beginning, the main part of the conversation will focus on, *What's better?* The chances are that something has been better for them at some time between the sessions. Asking the question can enable the student to recall what it is. If any suggestion made in a previous session has been left undone, one can assume it was just not helpful for them at that time.

In most cases students will rate themselves higher on the scale and this will help them recall other signs of progress. Similar strategies to the first session are used to amplify these by continuing to be curious and asking for more details, specific examples, other person perspectives, describing a video-recording and so on.

I: Hi there! I'm pleased to see you again … How did Manchester get on this week-end?

S: Hi! They won!

I: Oh good! Well now, let's see … What's better since I saw you last?

S: It's been okay …

I: Good! That's great … What's been okay?

S: I've been happier …

I: Good for you … excellent! Let's look at the scale … last week it was about a 4, right? *[Nods]* Where are you now, do you think?

S: I am a 6 now.

I: Wow, that's fantastic! What have you been doing that tells you you're a 6 now?

The point on the scale can be related to the aim, as in: *Where is it on the scale now?* and at other times to the person: *Where are you on the scale now?* I tend to personalise the rating whenever there has been progess.

Occasionally, the position on the scale may go down. If there have been any setbacks, the session will begin by asking coping questions to amplify how they managed to stop it from going down further, or kept it as high as they did.

> I: … Last week it was about a 4, right? *[Nods]* Where are you now, do you think?
>
> S: About a 3 …
>
> I: Ah, 3, that's understandable, given the difficulties you've had. How did you manage to make it stay there, and not go even lower?
>
> S: I tried not to let them bother me.
>
> I: Good for you! You tried to not let them bother you? How did you manage to do that?

Once any difficulty has been fully acknowledged, it is possible to gently put it to one side and still ask: What's been better? It is perfectly feasible that there have been some quite good times, or exceptions, even when the point on the scale has gone down. If the question is not asked, the student may not get the chance to talk about them.

> I: Hmm … so although there's been some tough times … you managed to cope with that very well. So, putting that aside a moment … What's been better?
>
> S: I've been getting on with my work … I got another certificate in Maths …
>
> I: That's fantastic … How did you get a certificate?
>
> S: I got all my work done …
>
> I: Yeah? That's excellent … What did the teacher say?

As progress is being made, the aim of the interviewing needs to be kept in mind to help the student recognize when the outcome they wanted has been achieved, at least to a satisfactory degree.

> I: I am so pleased with all that you have managed to do to make yourself happier in school … I'm wondering … where will you be on the scale when you think you won't be coming to see me any more?
>
> S: About an 8 …
>
> I: Ah, good! So when you are an 8 … what will be different about you then?

S: They won't be bothering me at all.

I: Yes, okay, I can see that ... and how will you be different then?

Most students do not need to rate themselves 10 on the scale before they are satisfied with life in school. More often than not, the sessions will end when they are a 7 or 8.

**Final session**

Any solution-focused session should be approached as if it might be the last, but there are ways of building resilience that are particularly appropriate in the final session, if they have not been covered earlier. Students can be invited to predict how they will use what they know now to keep or get themselves back on track, should similar difficulties arise in the future.

I: What tells you that you can manage to keep this up ... being happy in school now?

S: I think I'm not so worried now ...

I: Yes, that's great! And not being so worried, how does that help you?

S: I don't let things bother me so much ...

I: I'm wondering ... if things start to bother you one day ... how confident are you that you can stop worrying and get yourself back on track?

S: Yeah ... I'm fine now!

The final session can help students reflect on their own strengths and competencies, including what they have learned about themselves in managing to get where they wanted to be. Assisting them to appreciate what they have done builds their self-reliance for the future.

I: I'm so glad you're an 8 now – and I'm confident you will be fine – you have done so much, you deserve to be as happy as you are now in school. What do you think you have done that has helped you most?

S: Just ... err ... doing want I want to do, I suppose ...

I: Really! That's interesting! Such as ...?

S: If I want to talk to somebody, I just do it. It doesn't matter what others think …

I: You're right, that's great! What else?

Once the student is moving up the scale and life in school is more like they want it to be, the sessions should finish. As soon as possible, once the student reaches the aim of the sessions, or is confident that they can soon manage to do their own, the helper should get out of their way. According to de Shazer the number of sessions should be 'enough and not one more'.

## A last session

This is a transcription from a fourth and final session, where Gail Holdorf is interviewing a 15-year-old student for the last time. This is a superb example how someone skilled at solution-focused interviewing can empower someone referred for being bullied to reach this point of helpful self-awareness:

GH: Its 8 or 9! Oh that's really good! How have you done that?

S: I'd say that, the same things as what I've been doing and I've also learned how to ignore them and just like, go along with them. If they say – 'Are you smiling?' … say … 'Yeah, have you got a problem with it?' You know, messing about with them.

GH: Right.

S: Right, and if they say anything – you just laugh it off.

GH: Right, and it works?

S: Things to look forward to …

GH: Yes?

S: Mates … stay around them, they support me.

GH: Yeah?

S: Ignoring.

GH: Yeah?

S: Mm, just like trying not to be there at the wrong time. Like, say there is an argument going on, try not to get involved.

GH: Yes, that seems a good idea… ignoring… not getting involved. Do you see yourself moving higher than 8/9, or are your happy to be …?

S: I should be, by the end of this week.

GH: Right! Where do you think you'll get to then, by the end of this week?

S: 10.

GH: 10! Oh right, okay! Good!

S: I think it's going to be a lot better. Because people are always *[...not clear...]*

GH: Okay, so obviously what you're doing is working ... obviously you've got things sorted out ...?

S: I sort of trust people now. I don't know why, but ...

GH: You do? Right ...

S: I never used to trust anyone. If I was mates with people, I never like used to trust them like, if they said, 'Do you want to come into town?' I wouldn't trust them, because I'd feel that they would probably just leave me ... but now I do.

GH: Right ... and how does that help, then?

S: I thinks that helps, because if you can put trust in someone then it shows they are there for you all the time, not just there for you when they're going to get brayed *[beaten up]* and stuff like that.

GH: Yes, I suppose it works two ways as well, does it? If they feel you trust them, then they trust you as well. It makes a better relationship. Yes, I can see that – oh yes, that's really good! Yes, excellent! Right, so do you feel that you are okay now? That you're there and you're okay?

S: Yeah!

GH: Yes, excellent! I don't think we need to...

S: ... So I think it was just like school goes ... 'cos I can be like that as well ... I have to admit, I could be ... mates with someone ... but then if I feel they've done something wrong, I can just kick off as well as them.

GH: So what do you think is better now then? Why do you feel you can cope now? What's different?

S: Because everyone is like, I can, say, walk down the corridor without being scared and trying to cut through when I see people. I can talk to people now.

GH: Right!

S: I know that I've got support by the teachers and my friends ... my mam and that lot. So I'd say it's alright.

GH: Good, I'm pleased. Well, I think you've done really well. You've got a lot of good strategies and they are obviously working.

S: Yes.

## Outcomes

In an evaluation of all the referrals to an anti-bullying project during one year, the outcome data from solution-focused interviewing was examined in some detail (Young & Holdorf, 2003). Gail Holdorf, anti-bullying coordinator at that time, conducted all the interviews included in the review. Three-quarters of these were with secondary school-age students. It was decided to use the students' own scaling, rather than parents' or teachers' opinions, to evaluate whether the outcome was successful. The criterion for success was that students had progressed to a point on the scale where they considered they no longer needed any support. Although this provided the most consistent means of measuring success, it meant that 26 single session interventions had to be discounted from the evaluation, even though many of these were considered successful. The outcomes from the remainder are shown here:

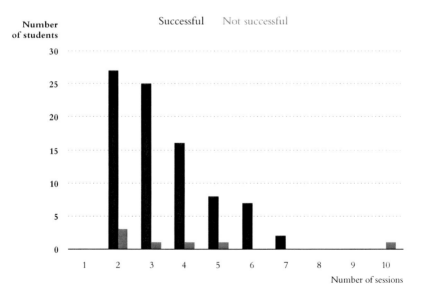

Outcomes: Solution-focused interviews

There were 92 cases that could be evaluated according to whether the pupils made progress along their scale until they were happy in school. 85 (92%) were completed successfully and the average number of sessions was 3.4 for these cases. The outcome was designated as 'not successful' where students did not reach a point where they felt they no longer needed support. In these seven cases, some students had nevertheless made progress on their scaling and none were lower on their scale than when they started.

As a rough guide, the first session with a student usually takes 30 minutes and subsequent sessions about 15 minutes each. Generally speaking, the second session would be arranged for about a week after the first. From then on, periods between sessions can lengthen depending on whatever the student thinks would be most helpful.

Although solution-focused interviewing provides very effective support for a student, there may continue to be incidents of bullying that need to be dealt with by the school staff, as usual. An intervention such as this operates in addition to, rather than replacing, the normal measures taken by the school in response to bullying.

### 'Ben'

Ben's mother and father were worried that their son had become withdrawn and his attitude had changed since going to secondary school. His work at school had deteriorated. They thought he was maybe smarter and cleaner than 'the average kid' at the school. He did have friends at school but his parents believed he possibly brought trouble upon himself sometimes by the way he behaved towards them.

The teacher said that Ben had been attacked in school and that, for example, on one occasion he had been pushed to the floor in a corridor and kicked repeatedly by several others. Police had twice been informed of nasty incidents, although no further action had been taken. He had been moved into another class but his teacher was worried that they did not seem to be able to protect him, particularly at lunchtime and between lessons. He had been allowed to go home the previous week, after the latest incident. There had been no apparent difficulty in his previous school. The teacher thought he was isolated and needed his confidence boosting.

When I saw Ben he said he wanted to be able to 'get on with his life'. Where 10 was *getting on with his life,* and 1 was *the worst it could be*, he scaled himself at a 5. He told me about lessons he enjoyed and what was different about him during these lessons – he was smiling and enjoying his work. When breaktimes went well, he was usually walking around outside or playing games with others. I asked him to notice what else was happening when breaktimes were going well.

The next week, Ben said he was about a 4 (1 less) at *getting on with his life* – although he was happier in school. He had been playing games more with friends at breaktimes and had managed this by simply asking them if he could join in. He had also attended an after-school club with a friend. He put himself at a 6 for *getting on with life – in school.* I telephoned his mother to find out how she thought he was managing. She was cautious, but she thought he did seem less worried and he had not mentioned any problems in school that week.

The next session he placed himself at 7 for getting on with life in school. When asked how he had managed to do this, he said he had been talking more with his mother and this had contributed to his being happier in school. I arranged to see him two weeks later. Meanwhile, he was going to keep playing with his friends and he added that he would keep away from some places in school where he thought there might be trouble for him. I did not pursue why this might be; I just accepted that he knew it would be a good idea and complimented him for thinking of it.

In the fourth session he said he rated himself at 10 in school. He was continuing to play games at break and lunchtime and he was going out more with friends after school. He appeared happy and smiling. An unusual thing happened when we finished this fairly brief, final conversation. He turned back from the door and came over and said earnestly, 'Thank you very much for your help.' I was very touched by this, although it is not something I would actively seek or encourage. The aim is to work 'leaving no footprints' (De Jong & Berg, 2008). I phoned his mother who seemed assured that he was much happier now in school.

### 'Shane'

Shane was in his first year at secondary school, referred by a member of staff because his mother was so concerned. By chance, a teacher who wanted to observe solution-focused interviewing was shadowing me. This offered another perspective that was not normally available. We went to see the mother at home first, as was usual when a parent raised concerns.

The mother felt her son was too shy to stick up for himself and he needed to 'come out of himself' and mix more with other children. She felt he was being picked on because he was so quiet. He was well behaved at home but had begun to lack interest generally and did not talk about school at all. However, she said he had been away one weekend with the geology club at school. In her view, he was about average academically and he was considerate to others. In the previous term he had been kicked in the head by another student and a teacher had interrupted this confrontation. His mother thought that it was unlikely that he would have retaliated – he would have just taken any aggression from others. However, at home he did stand up for himself and recently he had hit his sister. One day at school some girls took a chocolate bar off him and called him names. His mother became upset as she talked and said that she had been depressed lately, for unspecified reasons.

The impression of my observer was interesting. After leaving the interview with mum, she said this was clearly a difficult case and could not see what I could be expected to do – she seemed to be trying to reassure me, anticipating that this referral would be unlikely to have a successful outcome.

When we saw Shane in school, he put himself at 5 on the scale, where 10 was *happy in school* and 1 was *the worst it could be*. He was very quiet and spoke softly and slowly, head bowed, sometimes looking quite distressed. Even though we did not talk directly about any incidents, he did say at one point, 'Others [students] know I'm weak'. He had a friend in school that he often talked to at breaks and lunchtimes. He would prefer to be playing football and have more friends. His friend probably liked the fact that he talked to him and played board games with him in the games-room at break. Shane thought he had had a good morning on that particular day and he could tell me how he had managed this by talking to a number of other students. He thought that by talking more, to more people, things might get better. So I suggested he keep doing this and arranged to see him the following week. After the session, the observer remained pessimistic.

The following week as we waited in reception, Shane passed by with the class register and called out, smiling and saying, 'Hello'. The observer was surprised that he appeared so much brighter. When I interviewed him, he told me several things he had been doing, including talking to others and playing football – he and his friend had both been welcomed into the team. He had also been eating his lunch with other students. He and his friend had been talking more to other students and making more friends together. He rated himself at a 7 now. He thought his friend was happier too.

More remarkable than anything Shane said was the change in his general demeanour. He was sitting up straight, head up, talking quite freely and smiling at times. The observer who sat slightly behind him was (like me) visibly moved by this apparent turnaround and was even occasionally drying her eyes. Sometimes, in a case like this, it is extremely moving to see a child so much happier in such a short space of time. The observer left our meeting and went straightaway to her manager to ask if she could go for solution-focused training as soon as possible.

Inevitably not all referrals go so well or as quickly. It is a subjective judgement how often this kind of response happens. I reckon that roughly four out of five students show clear progress after just one session and about one in five can be stunning.

## Pupils bullying others

Throughout the ten years or so of close involvement with an inner city anti-bullying project, referrals have been overwhelmingly of 'victims' of bullying rather than 'bullies'. Pupils who may be described as 'bullies' are more likely to be referred for a wider range of difficulties, maybe for aggressive or disruptive behaviour, where bullying other pupils may feature.

Under normal circumstances in school, when a pupil is referred to a senior teacher for bullying, time is usually at a premium. The teacher will want to spend the few minutes they have available in the most effective way possible. Even if a student denies bullying, or blames the other pupil, they can still be expected to change what they do:

I: Mrs Smith has asked me to speak to you because you have been bullying another student. Is that right?

S: I haven't ... it's not true ... *(or)* I was only having a laugh ... *(or)* It was just a game ...

I: Okay ... I'm wondering what will Mrs Smith needs to see, that would tell her this?

S: I don't know ... he shouldn't keep complaining about me ...

I: Right ... so what do you need to do to stop him complaining?

S: I could just stay away from him ...

I: Will that be difficult for you to do?

S: No.

I: How will you manage that?

S: I'll just stay away ... not go near him ...

I: That will be helpful, thank you. I'll want to see you again next week so you can let me know how you get on...

S: Okay.

If it is the case that a student does not deny bullying but considers they are justified, or at least uses this as an excuse:

I: Mrs Smith has asked me to speak to you because you have been bullying another student. Is that right?

S: He is such a pain ... he pesters me at breaktime ...

I: Hmm ... so what can you do about that?

S: He won't go away ... I just push him to make him go away ...

I: Ah, I see! So what else can you do, so you don't feel pestered and you don't get into trouble for pushing him?

S: I can ignore him I suppose ...

I: That will be better ... How will you manage to do that?

S: Just keep talking to my mates ...

I: Will that be difficult?

S: No.

I: Okay ... Why don't you try that and we'll see how you get on over the next couple of days?

And if the difficulty persists:

I: I understand there has been more trouble?

S: Yeah.

I: Okay … so I'm wondering what has to happen to stop this becoming even more serious?

S: I don't know …

I: I don't want to have to speak your parents/make you stand outside my room at breaktimes/exclude you … So I need you to think about what you are going to do to resolve this …

S: Okay.

I: What will you manage to do this afternoon, to keep yourself out of trouble?

S: I'll keep away from him.

I: That would certainly be helpful. Come and tell me later if you managed to do that, will you?

S: Yes, okay.

When a student is referred for more sustained support for behaviour difficulties, it is useful to distance the person from the problem and describe the referral as arising from 'concerns' or 'worries' about the student, rather than complaints.

I: Right, I have been asked to talk to you because some teachers are concerned about you. Did you know that?

S: Yeah.

I: I want to help make things better in school for you. Is that okay?

S: It's not me!

I: I see, may I ask you some questions?

S: I suppose so.

I: Thank you. If I am able to help at all, what will be better in school?

S: I wouldn't be in trouble. I wouldn't have to come and see you!

I: Okay, yes, you're right, that would be better … so what will your teachers be seeing, for them to think there's no need for you to come and see me?

S: They wouldn't be telling me off…

I: I see … not telling you off … is that something you want?

S: Yeah!

I: So ... how will you be different when teachers are not telling you off?

S: It will be okay, I'll be getting on okay ...

I: Right, that would be much better! So, to get an idea how far you are already ... On a scale of 1 to 10, where 1 is the worst it could get, all the teachers telling you off all the time, and 10 is you getting on okay in school, just as you want to be ... Where is it now?

S: About a 4.

I: Ah! That's not too bad then, what is helping make it a 4 and not lower down?

S: I get on okay with some teachers ...

From this point on the conversation can follow a similar pattern to any other solution-focused interviewing, describing the times when the student is more successful in school, how they manage to behave like that and identifying something that works for them that they can do more of in the immediate future. The conversation can be helpful without being dependent on a student admitting to anything in particular such as bullying; the conversation can simply concentrate on making life better.

When relationships with peers have been the concern, it is an area to be especially curious about and other-person perspectives are particularly useful. *What do significant others like about the interviewee? How does the student manage that? When the pupil is successful in friendships, how does he/she manage that?*

Whilst being supported in this way, any misbehaviour or bullying may require sanctions when necessary, according to the behaviour policy. In the end, students have to take responsibility for their behaviour and inevitably a few will be unable to control themselves at times, given there are often background circumstances beyond the control of school staff. Nevertheless, they can be assisted by questions that assume they *are* capable and ask precisely how they will manage to make things better for themselves.

## Further reading

There is a 'crib-sheet' of possible questions together with a corresponding record sheet included as Appendix B. Dr Ron Warner from Toronto University handed out similar sheets, copied back to back on A4 paper, during my first training in solution-focused interviewing and I appreciate his permission for me to pass on this idea. When I started using this approach, I found it invaluable to read through the questions just before an interview. The format of the record sheet helped me to stay solution-focused and I knew there were clues overleaf, in case I got stuck. Other people may find this helpful when initially trying to conduct solution-focused conversations.

*Briefer: A solution-focused practice manual* is an excellent and inexpensive, explanatory booklet with lots of practical suggestions, by Evan George, Chris Iveson, Harvey Ratner and Guy Shennan of BRIEF in London.

For a detailed and yet readable exposition of solution-focused interviewing, the best book to date is *Interviewing for Solutions* by Peter de Jong and Insoo Kim Berg.

For solution-focused ideas within a school context, I would recommend Solution-Focused Education by Kerstin Måhlberg & Maud Sjöblom. They have also produced a very good DVD on class coaching, with English subtitles.

Yasmin Ajmal's introduction in *Solutions in Schools* provides a brilliant, short summary and is followed by chapters describing various applications of solution-focused thinking to problems in schools. Linda Metcalf has also produced a series of books with lots of examples.

Ben Furman's *Kids' Skills* provides a step-by-step, solution-focused workbook to support younger children in changing their behaviour.

## Summary

This chapter has given an outline of how solution-focused techniques in interviewing can help children and young people identify how to bring about change in their lives so they can overcome difficulties and succeed at being more like the person they want to be at school. The characteristic features of any solution-focused work are the same, although fine-tuned and intensified in individual interviewing.

The recommended books and the crib sheet may help someone trying to teach themselves, but the only way to learn how to do solution-focused interviewing is to have a go and then keep practising. Many people see the advantages of talking in this way to students at the first attempt and are inspired to continue improving their skills, becoming more and more solution-focused in all areas of their work.

# CONCLUSION

Solution-focused conversations can be viewed as 'nothing but a bunch of talk' (de Shazer, 1994), yet choosing what we talk about and how we talk about it makes a profound difference when we want to facilitate change for the better.

De Shazer and his team made significant discoveries about how conversations could be deliberately crafted to bring about change and Coopperider drew similar conclusions when he was working with large organisations. Solution-focused ideas were fine-tuned within the context of problem-solving, since this is where change is most urgent, but they apply equally to helping achieve progress in the absence of any problems and as such can be thought of as 'potential-focused'. The far-reaching implications of working in this way can inform anti-bullying projects in schools and indeed any initiatives that are intended to support improvement.

Throughout this book attention has been drawn to the characteristics of conversations that have been shown to be the most helpful:
  − Describing the preferred future
  − Recognising the successful past
  − Appreciating existing strengths
  − Doing more of what works

Techniques such as scaling, future-focused questions and complimenting/appreciation can assist in the process. However, solution-focused practice goes beyond simply asking the right questions. Certain assumptions underpin solution-focused practice and apply at any level of intervention, whether working towards improvement for a whole school, or

for groups within it such as staff, pupils or parents, or simply for individuals. These assumptions include:
- Everyone is the expert in their own life
- Everyone already has skills and strengths to help them reach their potential
- Resistance is a sign that a strategy needs to change
- Small differences make all the difference

It has been suggested how conversations may be used to promote change within the context both of professional development and life in school. Schools reduce the incidence of bullying by focusing instead on the ethos the school wants to promote - a friendly, safe and supportive environment. Recognizing what the school has already achieved and appreciating how everyone has managed get that far encourages further progress. Ideas that emerge during solution-focused discussions subtly build on existing expertise in a way that may be unique in any given school. Effective leadership encourages all members of the school community to fulfil their potential by helping them identify precisely what they are already doing that works and enabling them to do more of it.

The same principles and assumptions were applied in Chapter 3, when working with groups of children and young people in the classroom. Engaging pupils in discussions about how they want relationships in their class to be and how they can manage to make it happen avoids the risk of focusing on and reinforcing the unacceptable behaviour teachers wish to reduce.

The effectiveness of anti-bullying projects has generally been evaluated in terms of a reduction in bullying. Since all schools experience bullying, in some sense they can only ever fail less badly on these measures. Once monitoring and evaluation concentrates on achieving a preferred future, schools can measure their success by the increasing presence of what they want to see happening instead. Reductions in bullying are a predictable consequence of these improvements.

The last three chapters moved from preventing to responding to actual incidents and explained how skilfully constructed conversations can assist groups of children and individual pupils when they are being bullied or bullying others. These strategies have been proven to be effective.

Using a solution-focused approach to address bullying, from whole-school development to indivual pupil complaints, gives the added value of internal coherence and direction to a school's anti-bullying practice.

Governments are under constant pressure to respond to public concerns by improving services. They bring about change by passing new laws, diseminating guidance and monitoring performance. Bullying in schools provides a typical example of this. Whenever initiatives target a reduction in something that is not wanted, they risk increasing the problem. They impose additional work that may also lead to practitioner resistance. It is now being recognized that most traditional anti-bullying projects have lacked effectiveness and sustainability. Instead of continuing to blame the lack of commitment in schools, the overcrowded curriculum or the proliferation of other initiatives, we should 'do something different'. Schools' resistance is something to be learned from, not something that needs to be over-come.

Steve de Shazer and Insoo Kim Berg found the vital clues to effec-tiveness were already there – when they were successful with their clients in the therapy room – rather than derived from theories about clients or their problems. Cooperider found that in large organisations workers already know best when they do a good job and how they can do more of it.

The findings from anti-bullying projects increasingly support the belief that the means to reduce bullying are to be found within schools rather than inferred from theories about bullying. Once expertise about the problem loses its attraction as providing the basis for change, atten-tion can be turned towards recognising the school community as a more valuable resource for identifying effective, evidence-based prac-tice.

Identifying good practice and how it can be encouraged has impli-cations for research, support services, and government policies designed to bring about improvements, such as a reduction in bullying. Effective guidance 'leads from behind', helping schools detect and appreciate the knowledge and skills that many teachers and pupils use routinely, often without even realising it.

When research and consultancy follow a solution-focused path, the process of information gathering, measuring and reporting on the findings assists in bringing about the changes schools want. Only then can the call for more funding for anti-bullying initiatives be justified.

Schools are at their most effective when using their available skills and strengths to the full, in activities that build social cohesion and responsibility across the school community. They can use their considerable expertise to recognize when new ideas are helpful and to resist wasting effort on those that are not. Teachers can also foster supportive, cooperative relationships in the classroom by using the best of their existing curriculum and behaviour management skills. Carefully crafted conversations enable pupils to make their lives in school more like they want them to be.

Keys to unlocking the potential in schools can be found in the principle features and assumptions that underpin solution-focused practice.

# APPENDICES

These pages may be copied for personal use.

**Appendix A**
A simple live action plan

**Appendix B**
An example of a peer support group record sheet.

**Appendix C**
A 'crib-sheet' of suggested questions with a record sheet.

| Live Action Plan for .................................................................... | | |
|---|---|---|
| **Preferred future** | **Successful past** | **Strengths and skills** |
| What do we want? On a scale of 1-10, where are we now? | What makes it so high? | How did we do it? How are people involved? |
| Pupils getting along better in the breaks | Activities at break and lunchtime | Student council suggested break equipment/ activities |
| | Supervision at breaks and lunchtimes | X takes music club Y runs computer club |
| | | Everyone does break duty |
| | | Lunchtime supervisors |
| Cooperating with each other – in lessons | Teaching the personal and social curriculum, | Z gave training in circle time |
| Fewer complaints: (Instead?) Good relationships with parents | Dealing quickly with minor concerns | Senior teachers available to see parents |
| | School camping trip | Parents helping with camping and after-school football |

| Better peer relationships | |
|---|---|
| **More of what works** | |
| When we are one point further up the scale, what will be different? | How do we do that?<br><br>Responsibity and timescale? |
| More pupils involved in activities | Ask older pupils how they could help – maybe with lunchtimes/activities:<br> Y will ask his class for suggestions |
| Older pupils helping younger ones | X will put it on next student council agenda |
| Lunch supervisors more confident | Ask lunch supervisors what they want to happen more:<br> Dep Head, this week |
| Cooperative activities in lessons | Planning to include more cooperative activities:<br> Z will circulate ideas next week |
| More parents helping | Ask parents if they would like to help with activities:<br> Headteacher, put it in next newsletter |

| Support Group Record | | |
|---|---|---|
| Date:<br>**5 April** | Pupil/student to be supported:<br>**Sam** | |
| | Support group:<br>**Amed**<br><br>**Ben**<br><br>**Carl**<br><br>**Danny**<br><br>**Ethan**<br><br>**Freddie** | Suggestions:<br>**talk to him if he is on his own**<br><br>**sit with him at lunch-times**<br><br>**tell him some jokes**<br><br>**share some sweets**<br><br>**sit with him at lunch-times**<br><br>**playing with him at playtime** |
| **12 April** | Review with pupil/student:<br>**Fine – talking with Carl and Amed** | |
| | Review with group:<br>**Okay now, playing football, calling for him, looks happier.<br>F told someone to stop calling him names – will review.** | |
| | Review with pupil/student: | |
| | Review with group: | |
| | Review with pupil/student: | |
| | Review with group: | |

| **Support Group Record** | |
|---|---|
| Date: | Pupil/student to be supported: |
| | Support group: Suggestions: |
| | Review with pupil/student: |
| | Review with group: |
| | Review with pupil/student: |
| | Review with group: |
| | Review with pupil/student: |
| | Review with group: |

# Solution-focused interviewing: sample questions

**After most of these questions**
*What else?*

**Getting Started**
*What are you good at? What do you enjoy doing? If not self-referred: Your mum, teacher etc. is worried about you. Did you know that? I would like to help, is that ok?*

**Aims**
*What would you like to be better? What do you want? How will you know if this session has been useful to you? What is it you would like to change? What will make things better for you? If the goal is described as an absence of something: What will you be doing different/instead? and How would this help you? How would you prefer to be? Or if referred by someone else: What would s/he have see to know coming here was helpful? How would you know if s/he thought things were better?*

**Scaling**
*On a scale of 1 to 10, where 10 is just how you want to be and 1 is the worst you could imagine it being, where would you rate yourself right now?*

**Successful past**
*How did you manage to get to there? What makes you there and not one less? Can you give me an example? When things were a bit better? Implying skills and strengths: How have you managed to do this already? What is different about you now? What does your/ teacher/friend/parent notice? When else do you feel more ... happy/confident/how you want to be? How did you do that?*

**Coping(If 1 on the scale, or lower than the previous session)**
*How have you managed to cope so far? How else do you cope? How are you stopping things getting any worse? What gives you the strength to keep going? Where does that strength come from?*

**Preferred future**
*How will you know when it is 1 more on the scale? What will be different when it is a +1? What will you be doing differently?*

*What will I see on a video that will tell me you are a +1? How will you manage to do that? Who will be the first to notice? What will your teacher/mum/friend notice? How will this be important to you?*

**Miracle question**
*A strange question ... you go to sleep tonight as normal ... and during the night a miracle occurs, everything is just how you want it to be. When you wake up, tomorrow, you don't know. What is the first thing you notice? What are you doing differently? Who else notices? What do others notice? What's next? Small signs of the miracle: Has this happened before? ... a little bit? ... occasionally? Alternatively: imagine tomorrow you have a really good day ... what is the first sign that tells you this is a good day? What next? What's different about you?*

**Closing Phase**
**Aim**
*So you want to be ... more ...*

**Skills and strengths**
*I am impressed by ... I notice how ... You already ...*

**More of what works**
*Between now and the next time ... notice what is happening when it is a +1? Notice what you are you doing when it is +1? What will you be doing more ...? Can you experiment with doing more of ...? How soon will you be able to do/manage this? ... How soon will you be a +1? Will it be helpful for you to tell me how you are getting on? How long do you want before coming again?*

**Next session**
**Begins with**
*What's better?*

**Final session**
**Includes resilience questions**
*What gives you confidence for the future? When you have a setback, what will you be doing to get back on track? What tells you, you can cope well even with a setback?*

**Name:**                          **Session No.**          **Date:**

**Getting Started:**

_____

**Aim:**


**Scaling:**          1                                                          10
                    _____

**Successful past:**
**(Coping)**




**Preferred future:**




**(Miracle Question)**

_____

**Closing Phase:**
**Aim/Skills and strengths/More of what works:**




_____

**Next session: What's better?**

_____

**Final session:  Resilience**

# REFERENCES

Ainscow M. & Tweddle D. A. (1979) *Preventing Classroom Failure.* London: Fulton.

Ajmal Y. (2001) Introducing solution-focused thinking, in Y. Ajmal & I. Rees (Eds) *Solutions in Schools.*

Ajmal Y. & Rees I. (Eds) (2001) *Solutions in Schools.* London: BT Press.

Annis Hammond S. (1996) *The Thin Book of Appreciative Inquiry.* Texas: Kodiak Consulting.

Berg I. K. (2nd Ed 1999) *Family Preservation: A brief therapy workbook.* London: BT Press.

Craig C. (2009) *Well-being in Schools: The curious case of the tail wagging the dog?* Scotland: Centre for Confidence and Wellbeing.

DCSF (Department for Children, Schools & Families) *Bullying: A charter for Action.* Online, accessed April 2009. http://www.teachernet.gov.uk/wholeschool/behaviour/tacklingbullying/antibullyingcharter/

DCSF (2007, 2008) *Safe to Learn.* Online, accessed April 2009. http://www.teachernet.gov.uk/wholeschool/behaviour/tacklingbullying/safetolearn/

DCSF (2007) *SEAL: Social and Emotional Aspects of Learning.* Online, accessed April 2009. http://nationalstrategies.standards.dcsf.gov.uk/inclusion/behaviourattendanceandseal

De Jong P. & Berg I. K. (3rd Ed. 2008) *Interviewing for Solutions.* CA: Brooks/Cole.

de Shazer S. (1982) *Patterns of Brief Family Therapy.* New York: Guilford.

de Shazer S. (1985) *Keys to Solution in Brief Therapy.* New York: Norton.

de Shazer S. (1988) *Clues: Investigating Solutions in Brief Therapy.* New York: Norton.

de Shazer S. (1991) *Putting Difference to Work.* New York: Norton.

de Shazer S. (1994) *Words Were Originally Magic.* New York: Norton.

de Shazer S. & Dolan Y. with Korman H., Trepper T., McCollum E. & Berg I. K. (2007) *More than Miracles: The State of the Art of Solution-focused Brief Therapy*. New York: Haworth Press.

DFE (Department for Education) (1994) *Bullying: Don't suffer in silence. An anti-bullying pack for schools*. London: HMSO.

DFEE (Department for Education and Employment) (2000, 2002) *Bullying: Don't suffer in silence. An anti-bullying pack for schools*.

PricewaterhouseCoopers (2007) *Anti-bullying Alliance Evaluation Report*, DFES, Online, accessed April 2009. http://www.dcsf.gov.uk/rsgateway/DB/RRP/u014987/index.shtml

Durrant M. (1995) *Creative Strategies for School Problems*. New York: Norton.

Furman B. & Ahola T. (2006) *The Twin Star Book: A handbook of solution focused leadership and communication*. Helsinki Brief Therapy Institute.

Furman B. & Ahola T. (2007) *Change through Cooperation: Handbook of re-teaming, the art of motivating people to change what they want to change*, Helsinki Brief Therapy Institute.

Galloway D. & Roland E. (2004) Is the direct approach to reducing bullying always the best? in P. K. Smith et al. (Eds) *Bullying in Schools: How successful can interventions be?*

George E., Iveson C. & Ratner H. (2nd Ed 1999) *Problem to Solution: Brief therapy with individuals and families*. London: BT Press.

George E., Iveson C., Ratner H. & Shennan G. (2009) *Briefer: A solution-focused practice manual*. London: BT Press.

Goleman D. (1996) *Emotional Intelligence*. London: Bloomsbury.

Hallam S., Rhamie J. & Shaw J. (2006) *Evaluation of the Primary Behaviour and Attendance Pilot*, Research Report RR717. London: DfES.

Harachi T. W., Catalano R. F. & Hawkins J. D. (1999) Canada, in P. K. Smith et al. (Eds) *The Nature of School Bullying: A cross-national perspective*.

Hargreaves D. H. (2001) A capital theory of school effectiveness and improvement, *British Educational Research Journal*, 27, 4, 487-503.

Hillel V. & Smith E. (2001) Empowering students to empower others, in Y. Ajmal & I. Rees, *Solutions in Schools*.

Jackson P. Z. & McKergow M. (2002) *The Solutions Focus: The simple way to positive change.* London: Nicholas Brealey.

Koivisto M. (2004) A follow-up survey of anti-bullying interventions in the comprehensive schools of Kempele in 1990-98, in P. K. Smith et al. (Eds) *Bullying in Schools: How successful can interventions be?*

Limber S. P., Nation M., Tracy A.J., Melton G. B. & Flerx V. (2004) Implementation of the Olweus Bullying Prevention Programme in the Southeastern United States, in P. K. Smith et al. (Eds) *Bullying in Schools: How successful can interventions be?*

Macdonald A. (2007) *Solution-Focused Therapy: Theory, research & Practice.* London: Sage.

Måhlberg K. & Sjöblom M. (2004, Swedish 2002) *Solution-Focused Education.* Stockholm: Måhlberg & Sjöblom.

Måhlberg K. & Sjöblom M. (2008) *Lip-Focus: Feedback and Coaching to Develop the School.* DVD. Stockholm: Måhlberg & Sjöblom.

Maines B. & Robinson G. (1992) *The No Blame Approach.* Bristol: Lame Duck.

Mall M. & Stringer B. (2001) Empowering students to empower others, in Y. Ajmal & I. Rees (Eds) *Solutions in Schools.*

Mellor A. (1999) Scotland, in P. K. Smith et al. (Eds) *The Nature of School Bullying: A cross-national perspective.*

Metcalf L. (1995) *Counseling Toward Solutions.* New York: The Centre for Applied Research in Education.

Metcalf L. (1999) *Teaching Toward Solutions.* New York: The Centre for Applied Research in Education.

Molnar A. & Lindquist B. (1989) *Changing Problem Behaviour in Schools.* San Francisco: Jossey Bass.

The Office for National Statistics (UK) (2004) *Survey of the mental health of children and young people in Great Britain.*

The Office of the Children's Commissioner for England (2006) *Bullying Today.*

Ofsted (Office for Standards in Education) (2003) *Bullying: effective action in secondary schools,* London: HMSO.

Olweus D. (1999) Norway, in P. K. Smith et al. (Eds) *The Nature of School Bullying: A cross-national perspective.*

Olweus D. (2004) The Olweus bullying prevention programme: Design and implementation issues and a new national initiative in

Norway, in P. K. Smith et al. (Eds) *Bullying in Schools: How successful can interventions be?*

Ortega R, Del Rey R. & Mora-Merchan J. A. (2004) SAVE model: An anti-bullying intervention in Spain, in P. K. Smith et al. (Eds) *Bullying in Schools: How successful can interventions be?*

Pepler D., Smith P. K. & Rigby K. (2004) Looking back and looking forward: implications for making interventions work effectively, in P. K. Smith et al. (Eds) *Bullying in Schools: How successful can interventions be?*

Pepler D. J., Craig W. M., O'Connell P., Atlas R. & Charach A. (2004) Making a difference in bullying: evaluation of a systemic school-based programme in Canada, in P. K. Smith et al. (Eds) *Bullying in Schools: How successful can interventions be?*

Peterson L. & Rigby K. (1999) Countering bullying at an Australian secondary school with students as helpers, *Journal of Adolescence*, 22, 481–492.

Pikas A. (2002) New developments of the shared concern method, *School Psychology International*, 23, 3, 307–326.

Pikas A. (1989) The Common Concern Method for the treatment of mobbing, in E. Munthe & E. Roland (Eds) *Bullying: An international perspective*, London: Fulton.

Rhodes J. & Ajmal Y. (1995) *Solution Focused Thinking in Schools: Behaviour, reading and organisation*. London: BT Press.

Rigby K. (1997) *Bullying in Schools: And what to do about it*. London: Jessica Kingsley.

Rigby K, Smith P. K. & Pepler D. (2004) Working to prevent school bullying: Key issues, in P. K. Smith et al. (Eds) *Bullying in Schools: How successful can interventions be?*

Rosenbluth B., Whitaker D. J, Sanchez E. & Valle L. A. (2004) The Expect Respect Project: preventing bullying and sexual harassment in US elementary schools, in Smith P. K. et al. (Eds) *Bullying in Schools: How successful can interventions be?*

Salmivalli C. (2002) Is there an age decline in victimization by peers at school? *Educational Research*, 44, 3, 269–277.

Salmivalli C, Kaukiainen A. & Voeten M. (2005) Anti-bullying intervention: Implementation and outcome, *British Journal of Educational Psychology*, 75, 465–487.

Sharry J., Madden B. & Darmody M. (2003) *Becoming a Solution Detective*. New York: Haworth.

Shennan G. (2003) Solution-focused practice with families, in B. O'Connell & S. Palmer (Eds) *Handbook of Solution-Focused Therapy*, London: Sage.

Shilts L. (2008) The WOWW programme, in P. De Jong & I. K. Berg (3rd Ed.) *Interviewing for Solutions*.

Smith J. D., Schneider B. H., Smith P. K. & Ananiadou K. (2004) The effectiveness of whole-school antibullying programs: a synthesis of evaluation research, *School Psychology Review*, 33, 4, 547-560.

Smith J. D., Cousins J. B. & Stewart R. (2005) Antibullying interventions in Schools: Ingredients of effective programmes, *Canadian Journal of Education*, 28,4, 739-762.

Smith P. K. & Sharp S. (Eds) (1994) *School Bullying: Insights and perspectives*, London: Routledge.

Smith P. K., Madson K. & Moody J. (1999) What causes the age decline in reports of being bullied at school? Towards a developmental analysis of risks of being bullied, *Educational Research*, 41, 267–85.

Smith P. K., Morita Y., Junger-Tas J., Olweus D., Catalano R. & Slee P. (Eds) (1999) *The Nature of School Bullying: A cross-national perspective*. London: Routledge.

Smith P. K., Sharp S., Elsea M. & Thompson D. (2004) England: The Sheffield Project, in P. K. Smith et al. (Eds) *Bullying in Schools: How successful can interventions be?*

Smith P. K., Pepler D. & Rigby K. (Eds) (2004) *Bullying in Schools: How successful can interventions be?* Cambridge University Press.

Stevens V., Van Oost P. & De Bourdeaudhuij I. (2004) Interventions against bullying in Flemish schools: programme development and evaluation, in P. K. Smith et al. (Eds) *Bullying in Schools: How successful can interventions be?*

Sullivan K., Cleary M. & Sullivan G. (2004) *Bullying in Secondary Schools: What it looks like and how to manage it*. London: Paul Chapman.

Sullivan K. (2000) *The Anti-Bullying Handbook*, NZ: Oxford University Press

Ttofi M. M., Farrington D. P. & Baldry A. C. (2008) *Effectiveness of Programmes to Reduce School Bullying: A Systematic Review*. Report prepared for The Swedish National Council for Crime Prevention.

Whitney I., Rivers I., Smith P. K. & Sharp S. (1994) The Sheffield Project: Methodology and findings, in P. K. Smith & S. Sharp (Eds) *School Bullying: Insights and perspectives.*

Young S. (1998) The support group approach to bullying in schools, *Educational Psychology in Practice,* 14, 1, 32-39.

Young S. (2001) Solution focused anti-bullying, in Y. Ajmal & I Rees, *Solutions in Schools.*

Young S. (2002) *Solutions to Bullying.* Tamworth: NASEN.

Young S. & Holdorf G. (2003) Using solution-focused brief therapy in referrals for bullying, *Education Psychology in Practice*, 19, 4, 271-282.

Young S. (2008) Solutions for bullying in primary schools, in P. De Jong & I. K. Berg (3rd Ed.) *Interviewing for Solutions.*

# About the Author

Sue Young is now an independent consultant in solution-focused practice after working most of her career as a teacher in Hull, England. She began specialising in behaviour support in the early 1990s after completing a Master's degree in Pupil Behaviour at Hull University. As anti-bullying coordinator for Hull, her project on promoting friendship for classes in local primary schools was featured in the Times Educational Supplement and UNESCO's education newsletter. Her first training in solution-focused work was with Ron Warner in Durham in the mid 90's, and later in the first two on-line courses supervised by Insoo Kim Berg and Steve de Shazer, in Solution-Focused Therapy and Solution-Focused Supervision. She has since worked closely with Yasmin Ajmal and Guy Shennan from BRIEF in London and recently with Kerstin Måhlberg & Maud Sjöblom from FKC School in Stockholm. She contributes to the post-graduate course for Inclusion at Hull University and gives training in schools and presentations throughout Europe